Begging Dogs and Happy Pigs

Begging Dogs and Happy Pigs

Jason Clark

Blenheim Press Limited
Codicote

Published in 2009
by
Blenheim Press Ltd
Codicote Innovation Centre
St Albans Road
Codicote
Herts SG4 8WH
www.blenheimpressltd.co.uk

ISBN 978-1-906302-18-4

Typeset by TW Typesetting, Plymouth, Devon
Printed and bound by CPI Antony Rowe, Eastbourne

DEDICATION

To the people of Cuba who have persevered for so long
to uphold what they believe in.

CONTENTS

FOREWORD

Poet, artist, actor, adventurer, linguist, pedagogue; I've always found a means to express myself, though nowhere has inspired me as much as Cuba. Since my teens I have longed to go there. This fictional-biography is deeply personal, and moving. I intend to make you laugh at my own, too human follies and smile at my adventures. Funny, yes, but tragical mirth, as I slowly reveal what life is like in Cuba today. Political tension weighs on everyone and stomach bugs are rife.

My love for the Cuban people is always at the forefront of this factual story; where you will discover beautiful women, exotic locations and fat pigs. The relationships I developed there I will never forget and will always cherish. I wrote this book at the turning point of my life, a time of crisis and self-revelation, a time of intimacy and a discovery of inner beauty. This inner journey is as important and revealing as the outer journey.

I hope you will get as much enjoyment from my experiences in this fascinating country as I did and that this story will help you develop a greater awareness of another world.

INTRODUCTION

Cuba is probably the most beautiful prison in the world. It is a prison for its inhabitants and to some extent for people who stay there, and also because of its geographical situation and because of its politics. Cubans have everything that could be needed for a healthy community except freedom of movement – it's very difficult to leave Cuba – economic freedom (this is the main reason Cubans don't leave) and freedom of speech; people seemed genuinely frightened to speak out against their government.

Geographically, although the island has changed since Columbus arrived there in 1492, there are still some remnants of the tropical paradise he describes in his log book. Rare and tropical birds can still be found in what is left of the tropical forests. Parrots, humming birds, frigates, pelicans, harmless snakes and boa constrictors, spiders, crocodiles (Cuba sports the biggest species of crocs in the world) are all to be found there. The beautiful beaches outline the warm Caribbean and Atlantic seas that hold host to many reefs, the fourth largest in the world, black and red coral can be seen as well as many coloured fish, sharks, rays, dolphins etc . . .

The geographical and animal features do not alone make up the beauty of the country. The lack of industry and the relatively small number of cars means that it is a country with little pollution and very pure, fresh air, kept cleaner by the nearly constant breeze. The food is, as far as I know, all organic, as the use of pesticides ended when the imports from Russia stopped. Semi-wild mangoes, guavas, bananas, oranges and fresh sea food all add up to this purity little known to the industrialised countries.

Although the Arawaks may have died out the present inhabitants of the isle, often mixed Black African and Latino, are quite beautiful. And all the Cubans make an effort with their appearance, however poor. Music and dance abound throughout the country, there's little else to do, and the universal education means that most Cubans can engage in conversation to a reasonable level.

Not only has Castro's Communist government imposed equality on the population but it has also made it is a very safe country. There is little gun crime simply because there are few guns. Havana is reputed to have a policeman on every corner, it certainly seems that way in many areas. The strict penalties prevent drug trafficking and the fact that the people have so little disposable income means they can't afford to get drunk. Though alcohol abuse is one of the greatest social problems in Cuba.

This book was not intended to be a manifesto for Cuban tourism, nor was it intended to be a travel guide, there are plenty of those on the market, though many of them are quite dated now. No, originally this book wasn't intended as a book at all, it was quite simply a letter to my mother describing my stay in Cuba.

I don't particularly like travel writing, nor do I like travelling and tourism. My favourite travel writers are Laurence Sterne and Jack Kerouac and a small out of print book called *Une Excursion dans le Morvan 1892*. For me it is important to meet people, to live with people, to get to know and understand their culture and customs and even take part in them. There are a few facts in this book, but most of what I write is hearsay and rumour based on reports of friends of mine. Even what they had to say is often uncertain and contradictory, confused by the climate of paranoia typical of any communist society. From the views of these few choice friends I established my own opinion, opinions made to raise questions rather than to give answers. I encourage you to check any facts and figures and add them to the information given in this book.

Above all, this writing is about me, my time in a country I've wanted to visit most of my life and never got around to. I felt it was time to see Cuba now, as did many tourists I met while I was out there. I went to see a country in a state of crisis and on the brink of change and found that I was the one in the state of crisis.

The reasons I wanted to go to Cuba when I was sixteen are summed up in Ché's Farewell Letter to Fidel. I was impressed with the idealistic fervour of these people who, for so long, have got away with sticking the middle finger up to the USA. What kept these eleven million people going so long in spite of the international trade embargo forced upon them by the various presidents of the USA? I could identify with a people fighting for an ideal as I had fought for my own beliefs (as a Steiner/Waldorf teacher) for ten long years. I consider myself as an anti-materialist in a similar way that I imagined the Cuban people to be anti-capitalist. I needed to see for myself if the myths, rumours and reports that stretched to Europe were true of this country led by a man who has survived two CIA assassination attempts. Rumours of ongoing revolution, of hardship and suffering in the name of an ideal seemed never ending.

I was fascinated, though not to the point of obsession (politics bores me), about this little country that has been at the centre of world history since 1492. I also wanted to go somewhere warm and swim in the warm sea.

The only reliable facts in this book are the events that I felt and witnessed myself, the only truths are those of my own emotions and thoughts. To a great extent this book is about me. It is necessary to explain a few facts about myself. My ethos is to leave the planet a better place than I found it. Most of my working life has been spent educating children in a way that I believe will help change the world for the better. I now live on a boat; a sailing boat, that I have restored myself using as much as possible recycled materials. The whole boat is recycled, that is to say it was going to rack and ruin and needed repairing. I'm trying to generate my own electricity and have cut my energy emissions by 80% by living on the boat. I am, of course, a vegetarian and have been for nearly twenty years. I believe in Freedom and I believe in Ecology and both these I find in my boat. I enjoy sailing. My sailing heroes are Tristan Jones and Bernard Moitessier whom I respect for their anti-corporate stance to sailing, who showed that heroes can still be heroes without sponsorship.

My main mission was to find a boat and sail back to Europe as crew, maybe via Jamaica or another Island in the Caribbean. I really wanted to get some transatlantic sailing experience before I attempted it, one day, in my own boat. It still remains a dream for me to sail across the Atlantic and Cuba still remains a destination I'd aim for, but then this is another story and depends a lot on me raising the finances to do the trip, another reason for writing this book.

The main reason for my stay in Cuba, or rather the pretext for me going there, was to improve my Spanish to a good enough level so that I could teach it as my second modern language. The dream, the mission and the reason all matched together perfectly and I found a language school that had teachers in Cuba. I also had a Cuban friend who would introduce me to his family and friends.

So what did I find in Cuba? Did I find an ideal to die for? No, rather I found a reason to live.

As for the Cuban people I met out there, they are tough. They are tougher and more resilient than any other people I've come across. Descendants of conquistadors and slaves, who stamped out the most terrifying cannibals of all times (and I sometimes wonder if there is something of the cannibal in the Cubans, they seem to be capable of eating anything), the strength of will of these people is very impressive. When I got to know them I found they were also among the kindest people I ever met. Kind but not always sympathetic, sympathy didn't appear to be part of their cultural make-up. If you were ill you were ill but once you recovered they were obviously grateful.

Once I'd made a friend there I was told, rather ominously, that I had a friend for life, and I feel this is the case. Cuban hospitality is extended to the family and close friends, everyone else is treated a little off-handedly and with a certain level of suspicion. But once you are welcomed into the family you are treated like a king, which can be a little overwhelming for some foreigners.

It's not surprising that families are so close knit when more often than not four generations of the same family would live under the same roof. Great grandparents, grandparents, parents and children would share bedroom, lounge, kitchen and bathroom. And the answer to your question is: they go outside for it or all the family sit in the garden or landing whilst amorous couples are left alone.

Cuba is a third world country, yet in the face of their poverty they always have something to give, and enjoy receiving. A couple of times I went into a house to be met by a child asking for *un regalo*. This seemed quite acceptable, at least for most of the people I met. Though as a tourist many waiters expect a tip and carry on asking for *un regalo* in a similar way to the children.

Nearly everyone has a decent level of education. I was told that to work in the cigar factories a worker has to be able to speak two foreign languages in order to be able to talk to visiting tourists and answer questions. It would be interesting to know who were the most educated factory workers in the world.

Religious tolerance is practised throughout the country. One can find Catholic, Protestant, Islamic, Jewish and many of the various derivations of these religions, practised in places of worship throughout the country. There is also an Afro-Cuban religion. The worship of Orishas is practised in many homes.

However, in spite of this religious tolerance and reasonable level of education I came across much racism in Cuba. Racism is ubiquitous and everybody fits into one of the three racial categories: Latinos (Cubans) Mulattos (Cubans) or Negroes (Cubans), each claiming to be more

Cuban than the others. This was one of the many surprises and contradictions I met. How could a country where the government preaches equality for all, a country that overcame and overthrew its roots, roots that were established on slavery, which was probably the centre pin of the slave trade for centuries, how could there still be social distinctions based purely on the colour of the skin? I saw very few black members of the communist party, a few Mulattos but mainly Latinos.

The only place that Cubans are really united is in their music, that extends from various ethnic origins: Afro-European and Caribbean. Music and dance mean everything to the Cuban and can be encountered everywhere. I believe salsa came to Cuba from New York in the 1970s, but it might have been the other way round. The best dancers I've seen were definitely the older people whose rhythm and movements stemmed directly from jazz.

Is this all about to change? There is an atmosphere of change, or at least a feeling of a need for change, although most people I spoke to wouldn't believe it is possible. Most foreigners, however, did. When I read the guide books before travelling out there some said that the Cubans would often complain, *no es facil*, and though I heard this a few times, mainly from older people who'd grown up during the pact with Russia, more commonly I heard the refrain *Algun dia*, one day . . . One day it will change. But how?

Today the society is, to some extent, schizophrenic. Two social systems exist simultaneously. Officially the society is communist, or as my friend A describes it, 'state-run capitalism'. What I found was a system that was quite simply anti-American. Whatever the Bush administration does is considered bad, therefore the Cuban government do it differently. The state controls everything and everyone is afraid of the police, though not of the policemen themselves. Nothing appeared clear and I met much confusion as to what is allowed and what isn't. This confusion reaches a state of paranoia when the police stop and search vehicles or inspect houses (*Casa Particular*) randomly and frequently. Nobody knows who is listening or what is safe to say. On more than one occasion I was asked not to repeat what I was being told.

Television only adds to the level of confusion. Cuban state TV continuously broadcasts government messages saying how bad the North American government is. The news bulletins are blatantly biased against the USA. Yet in spite of the continuous anti-American propaganda the best films on TV are American! *Die Hard I, II* and *III*, or many American feel-good-factor movies are shown, followed directly by a political discussion commenting on how bad American foreign policy is. One of the most popular TV series in Cuba is *The X Files*!

Probably nowhere is the dual society more apparent than in the monetary system. There are two types of currency in Cuba. The national money, that the Cubans earn and spend, which is called *Pesos*, *monnai nacional*, *Pesetas*, *dinero* ... and most commonly *Pesos Cubanas* or PC, notably the same initials as *Partidad Communista*. These can be used by anyone, but most people prefer *Pesos Convertibles*.

Pesos Convertibles, CUC (*Curuncia Universal de Cuba*), *Pesos*, *Pesos touristas*, or *dollars*, as they are most commonly called, were introduced to replace the American dollar which is used in most Latin American countries as a more stable currency than their own.

Pesos Convertibles are for foreigners bringing money in from abroad and are intended to be used in all the tourist resorts, bars and restaurants for tourists, taxis, buses for tourists etc. In fact unless you can get away with being a Cuban, Cubans rarely accept Cuban *Pesos* and invariably charge tourists over the odds using CUC. In 2007 one pound sterling equalled 1.79 CUC and there were 24 Cuban *Pesos* to a CUC.

A Cuban wishing to buy anything using CUC, and in some bars you could only buy cigarettes in CUC, would first have to change their Cuban *Pesos* to CUC in the bank. The only other source of gaining CUC is directly from tourists. Therefore most people want to work in the tourist industry.

Of course because of the complexity of the official system and the fact that the government doesn't provide all, as it claims to do, there is a huge black market. *El Marcao Negro* is probably the most popular system for trade and economy. Nearly everything runs on the black market as everybody is after that extra buck, but because most of the basics are provided for by the government; housing, basic foods, the infrastructure, refuse collection, street lights etc ... it doesn't take a lot to earn that bit extra. Being the black market of course there is no tax on the money they may earn. The greatest earner outside trade and barter is through dealing illegally with tourists. All Cubans do this, except of course, my friends who are all good upright citizens.

The sale of lobster is a good case for the black market economy. Every *Casa Particular* will offer lobster at some point. Though the people I stayed with wouldn't dream of breaking the law.

Officially lobster has to be bought and sold by the governmental market. This means travelling to the official market and paying ten times the price it was bought for, when it is easier to ask a neighbour fisherman to sell (or give) you a lobster for a couple of *pesos*. The price of lobster in a restaurant, owned by the government, is around 17 CUC. A *Casa Particular* would offer you one for as little as 5 CUC.

In the CP where I stayed, good Cuban citizens as they are, they wouldn't have thought of offering me lobster. Were I to mention eating such foods it would be unlikely that I ate it in the place I was staying. Equally I would not have wished to break the law by eating such clandestine foods and any mention of doing so probably refers to me eating in an officially recognised restaurant where the lobster was bought from a government source and not just fished directly from the sea.

Houses are bought and sold in a similar fashion, as I explain further on. Though not to tourists, well not directly anyway. There are many rumours of foreign investors and foreign residents securing properties in spite of the fact that no-one can own the houses they live in.

As confusing as all this may seem it appears quite clear to most Cubans, though some are more successful at exploiting the system than others. There is a new bourgeoisie growing in Cuba made up of those who are able to earn a disposable income from their contact with tourists. These people, mostly owners of *Casa Particulars*, can afford new clothes, holidays and building work to their houses, though they still aren't allowed to own their houses. Economically there is, ironically, a three tier system in Cuba. Although Castro famously stated that no member of the Cuban government has a dollar in his bank, they do alright for themselves. Castro is reported to have 52 houses. The top government officials live in luxurious houses in the Miramar area of Havana, alongside foreign diplomats and officials. The only Cuban yachts I saw were for the use of government officials who also drive the biggest cars and eat a lot of lobster. Next on the social scale come the officials who work with foreigners, tourist workers, international lawyers etc. They make up the middle classes and are the only people with some disposable income, though this is limited. Anyone seen to make too much money will soon have it taken off them. At the bottom of the scale is the poor majority, mainly black or peasants (by peasants I mean country workers, farm workers, tractor drivers etc) who live in wooden buildings often with poor sanitary conditions and go around barefoot so as not to wear out their shoes.

Obviously this leads to prejudice and jealousy and the poor dislike the middle classes who in turn are suspicious of the Civil Servants. However all the time I was in Cuba I never heard a bad word against Castro, who seems to be admired by all. While the government got a lot of discreet criticism, Ché has reached a level of idolism bordering on sanctity. He is seen by most Cubans as somewhere between a pop icon and a demi-god.

DISCLAIMER

Because of the level of paranoia, the genuine fear of reprisals by the police for speaking against the government or behaving illegally, and because I don't know the Cuban laws and it was often unclear to me whether my Cuban friends were breaking the law or not, I have to be very discreet when talking about the people I met there. To help keep their anonymity I will only use initials or nicknames I made up myself. I will also avoid all physical descriptions, which is a great shame because I would love to describe the people I met. The anonymity is because I am genuinely concerned that there may be misunderstanding and legal repercussions for my friends. I will also call my Cuban friend in England A. This is because he is going through the tricky process of becoming a British National and I wouldn't like this to be prejudiced in any way. There are no photos to go with this book, mainly because I broke my waterproof camera and dropped it in the sea, it leaked and ruined all the film. But most of the pictures you can find on Google Earth. They are a lot better than the pictures I would have taken anyway. Just click on Trinidad and you will see the town, the beach at Ancon, la Boca and just about most places I talk about.

Voltaire once said: 'I may not agree with what you say but I'm prepared to die to give you the right to say it' (my own translation).

In spite of the strange and vastly complicated relationship between America and Cuba (a relationship which once nearly led to the entire destruction of the planet), and maybe it is because of the complexity of this relationship, Cuba is politically a fascinating place. The American naval base in Guantanamo is symbolic of the political stalemate between the two countries. I apologise beforehand for my very simplistic view of the situation. The Cuban anti-imperialistic revolution is essentially against America. As long as the Americans remain in Cuba the Cuban government has to continue its communist revolution, and as long as the communist revolution continues in Cuba the American government will perceive Cuba as a political and military threat and will therefore, remain in Cuba. I can't see any way out for either side, as both the Cubans and the Americans are quick to label each other as terrorists. All I know is that my Cuban friends are very nice people as too are my American friends and I'm sure they would all get on very well if we were allowed to have a barbecue on the beach together.

Furthermore Cubans have had to do with so little mainly due to the trade embargo, and it would be nice to help them out a little, and we in the so called developed world have so much, too much really, I wonder where we put it most of the time.

Here is a list of ten things you can do, if you go to Cuba, to help beat the international trade embargo:

(1) Import useful things; umbrellas, puncture repair kits, tools of any description, cooler boxes, shoes, clothes, bed linen (no duvets or jumpers).
(2) Import fun things: marbles, balls, DVDs (be selective), chocolate.
(3) Import interesting things: books (be careful with anti-communist propaganda), magazines, encyclopaedias etc . . .
(4) Import necessary things: anything your local chemist sells, especially Nurofen, anti-diarrhoea treatments, condoms, tampons, sanitary towels etc.
(5) Spend your money freely once you get to Cuba.
(6) Drive to out of the way places and mix with the community. Introduce yourself by offering a few tools to a local farmer or craftsman. Give gifts to children. Teach them new games and sports.
(7) Don't exploit the people: many investors are sitting waiting to buy up property ready for when the revolutionary government changes. Salivate over but don't try to buy the old American cars (Cuba's greatest asset).
(8) Encourage organic farming: it's easier for Cubans to do this. Buy organic cotton clothes (very good quality and very cheap). Don't bother bartering.
(9) Smoke more: Yes I know but it is one of their main exports!
(10) Drink more rum: This helps everyone and after a while you no longer care about the embargo. 'Embargo, what embargo?'

There are many other groups supporting Cuba and many trying to bring down the present government. You can choose to join either of these or do nothing, like most people. Whether you are pro-Cuban, pro-

American or just like holidays in the Caribbean I can certainly say it is refreshing to live in a country with so little American influence.

Tourism has to be Cuba's greatest source of income today. The film *Buena Vista Social Club* was not only a film about some cool old men, who play groovy music, it also marked the opening of Cuba to the outside world. Still many people go today to Cuba for salsa. But most tourists go for other reasons, and Cuba has a long history of tourism that dates back a long time before the revolution. Tourism is mentioned in Hemingway's *The Old Man and the Sea*, and it would be too much to say that Columbus was the first trans-Atlantic tourist. Many tourists today still go with the attitude of the conquistador or the colonialist trying to get the most out of the natives, you can often see them bartering at artisanal markets or consuming the sights, clicking away with their digital cameras like Japanese tourists, out to get the best clichés. But the Cubans know this and will be extremely friendly and helpful in return for your money. One thing they're not used to, and that is foreigners coming for long term stays.

There are many tourists from all over the world, except of course the USA. An American caught going to Cuba may be arrested once they return to the USA and fined up to 250,000 dollars as well as facing five years in prison. This puts off most North Americans, though I did hear rumours of Americans coming to Cuba via Mexico or Venezuela, but these are probably Canadians. There are a lot of Canadian tourists in Cuba. I did see a few photos of Jack Nicholson in Havana so somehow he's found a way in and out, or maybe he just pays the fine! As far as I know the Cubans have no difficulties with Americans coming into the country as long as they are coming on holiday and not invading.

There are essentially three types of tourists who come to Cuba. Tourists come on package deals, mainly Canadians and Europeans, then there are travellers who are going around the world or travelling in Latin America, most of these are under 25, and then you can meet Eco/politico tourists who are there for the environment and because of the political make-up of the country. Strangely I didn't meet any tourists who just came for Eco tourism or just for the culture; they all seemed interested in both.

The activities that these tourists can enjoy are quite distinct, and though most people come for one specific reason, they would often dabble with some other aspect of tourism, things the Cubans wouldn't necessarily do or want to do.

The leisure industry was mainly established around the big foreign hotels (Ibirostar and Novotel) and included typical holiday activities such as swimming in pools, diving, sailing, horse riding, flying excursions etc … I only ever saw Germans in the big hotels unless they were anthropology students. Anthropology seems a good excuse to travel and as far as I can tell there are a lot of German anthropologists. Beach bumming seemed quite a popular activity among the younger (traveller) tourist, who would spend entire days lying on the beach or swimming in the sea. The more energetic ones would play volleyball. Dancing and music are big attractions for tourists who would regularly enroll for dance classes or bongo lessons, though this appears to be less popular than before. Many foreigners, mainly women, would come just for the dancing as they will always find a dance partner and invariably told me that Cuban men are the best dancers in the world. Various types of tourists come for the culture and nearly all were more interested in Ché and Fidel than the Modern Art Museum or the ballet.

There were also many foreign students who were interested in the political system. Eco-tourism is quite big and excursions to nature reserves seemed popular with all types of tourists, visits to see wild turtles, waterfalls or reefs were done by tourists from all walks of life. Although I heard that sex-tourism was quite big in Cuba I didn't see much of this practised overtly as is the case in many Latin American countries. What I did witness, over and over again, were many beautiful (and they were nearly always good looking) and wealthy (I could tell from the designer beach wear) young women who came to Cuba quite simply to fuck the men. Often, and I observed this at least ten times in Trinidad and heard mention of it in Havana, they would meet up with a young Cuban, nearly always black – black Negro, not black mulatto – and spend a week or two with him, taking him to expensive hotels, hanging around with him and his black friends. What surprised me the most was that these young ladies apparently from well-to-do families would not be allowed to behave like that in their own countries. In fact a few foreign women told me they felt a lot freer in Cuba than they did in their own countries. Of the young women going to Cuba for the men, I noticed they were predominantly Irish or Scandinavian, though some were Canadian. The only time I saw anyone kissing openly in the streets were foreign women kissing Cuban men. The opposite did not happen. Cuban women are far more discreet about their relationships with tourists because they don't wish to be branded as *puttas*. However they did have encounters with tourists that usually involved money being exchanged somewhere along the line, even if it didn't have the guise of overt prostitution. Many Italian men were in Cuba quite simply to be with black women.

As far as package tourism is concerned, if you want to go to a smart hotel on a golden sandy beach I don't see the point in travelling all the way to Cuba when there are just as pleasant beaches in Spain and on the Spanish islands.

Following various news reports, and according to Castro himself, Cuba has a developing ecological programme. They are installing wind generators and solar panels to generate electricity in the more secluded villages or areas it is difficult to get mains electricity to, however they are lacking the equipment to do so and rely on foreign imports.

There is at least one nuclear power station (built by the Russians) that I know of and this, as far as I know, is the main source of electricity on the island. There is no gas and little petrol because of the trade embargo, though outside of Havana there are few cars so they don't have a high fuel consumption. I believe they have no coal reserves and what is left of the natural woodland is protected. Without help from outside, and this help seems to be coming from China, North Korea and a few Latin American countries, Cuba would have an energy crisis.

There is a programme for ecology in Cuba but this seems to be being undermined by the black market. Lobsters are protected by the law but if all 11 or 12 million Cubans decided to eat lobster brought from the black market there would be few left.

There is a programme of development for organic farming and urban farming. Apparently there is more urban farming in Cuba than in any other country in the world. However this was brought about by the embargo rather than by any particular political programme for environmentally friendly farming. Because there is so little transport food had to be produced in or near towns or cities.

One can find *organoponicas* on the outskirts of most towns. An *organoponica* is like an allotment where organic food is grown and sold directly. The ones I saw offered a variety of foods, a greater variety than you can usually buy in the streets, where most fruit and vegetables are sold. However I was told that this food was expensive for most people.

As with the majority of third world countries water and sanitation is a problem. Though the government is aware of this and is working towards having sanitised water for everyone this is still a long way from the case.

I came across lots of cases of stomach illness when I was there and managed to have a stomach upset that lasted six weeks, every time I ate I had diarrhoea. Though everyone, including the doctors in England and France, thought at first I might have caught a *giardia* from drinking well-water, the tests showed nothing. It is probably more likely that I got gastro-enteritis from eating lobster, or it might have been the cat-fish or any other of the odd fish I ate out there.

There is very little industrialised food and most state-produced food is rationed. No-one is allowed to eat beef except children and old people, there is an egg ration and a bowlful of rice a day as well as bread and other basic foodstuffs.

Outside of Havana, urban composting is practised in most towns. The pig man comes by every other day to collect food waste. In fact very little is wasted in Cuba, bottles are re-used or saved for an emergency. Everything is repaired and kept going for years, many of the fridges date from before the revolution, as do the cars and lorries.

None of this environmentally friendly behaviour is due to any particular eco-political approach, it is quite simply due to the fact that Cubans have had to do without for so long that they are reluctant to throw anything away.

In fact if the whole world chose to live like Cuba the world would be a healthier, cleaner and safer place. Unfortunately even the Cubans don't chose to live the way they do. Their way of life is forced on them by the political regime and the international trade embargo forced on them by the US who refuses to deal with anyone who deals with Cuba. Though this seems like classroom politics, I'm sure most seven year olds could come up with a solution. But all this may change when Castro stands down from power, or when he dies.

This book is dedicated to all my friends in Cuba.

CHÉ'S FAREWELL LETTER TO FIDEL

HAVANA

Year of Agriculture (1965)

Fidel:

I remember many things in this hour – how I met you in the house of Maria Antonia, and how you proposed that I come with you, and all the strain of the preparations.

One day they passed by to ask who would be advised in case of the death, and the real possibility of it struck us all. Later we knew that it was true, that in a revolution one triumphs or dies (if it be a true one). Many comrades were left along the road to victory.

Today everything has a less dramatic tone, for we are more mature, but the event is repeating itself.

I feel that I have fulfilled the part of my duty that bound me to the Cuban Revolution on its territory, and I take my farewell of you, my comrades and your people who are now my people.

I formally renounce my posts in the leadership of the Party, my post as Minister, my rank as Major, my status as a Cuban citizen. Nothing legally binds me to Cuba, only ties of another kind that cannot be broken, as can official appointments. Looking back over my past life, I believe that I have worked with sufficient faithfulness and dedication in order to consolidate the revolutionary triumph. My only deficiency of any importance is not to have trusted you more from those first moments in the Sierra Maestra and in not having fully understood soon enough your qualities of leader and revolutionary.

I have lived through magnificent days and at your side I felt the pride of belonging to our people in the luminous and sad days of the Caribbean Crisis. Rarely has any statesman shone more brilliantly than you did in those days. I feel pride, too, in having followed you without hesitation, identifying myself with your way of thinking and seeing and of judging dangers and motives.

Other regions of the world claim the support of my modest efforts. I can do what is forbidden to you because of your responsibility to Cuba, and the time has come for us to separate.

Let it be known that I do it with a mixture of joy and sorrow: I am leaving here the purest of my hopes as a builder and the most loved among my beloved creatures, and I leave a people who accepted me as a son; this rends a part of my spirit. On new battlefields I will carry with me the faith that you inculcated in me, the revolutionary spirit of my people, the feeling of having fulfilled the most sacred of duties: to fight against imperialism wherever it may be; this comforts and heals any wound to a great extent.

I say once more that I free Cuba of any responsibility save that which stems from its example: that if the final hour comes upon me under other skies, my last thought will be for this people and especially for you, that I am thankful to you for your teaching and your example, and that I will try to be faithful up to the final consequences of my acts; that I have at all times been identified with the foreign policy of our Revolution, and I continue to be so; that wherever I may end up I will feel the responsibility of being a Cuban revolutionary, and I will act as one; that I leave nothing material to my children and my wife, and this does not grieve me: I am glad that it be so; that I ask nothing for them, since the State will give them sufficient to live and will educate them.

I would have many things to say to you and to our people, but I feel that they are unnecessary; words cannot express what I would want them to, and it isn't worthwhile wasting more sheets of paper with my scribbling.

To victory forever. *Patria o Muerte!*

I embrace you with all my revolutionary fervour!

CUBA

HABANA

Day 1

Arrived on Sunday, *Fiesta de Las Madres*. The Cubans know how to do Mother's Day: salsa blasting from every rooftop, dancing in the streets. Thumping raga and salsa blasted from most apartments, people were dancing in the streets and balconies looked as though they would collapse under the weight of dancing families. Everywhere there was movement, all to the rhythm of the music. Cool cars, Cadillacs and old 1950s American cars (though not too many) cruised slowly along the coastal road and wound their way through the barrios, the same music blasting out of tired speakers. There are as many Ladas and other Russian made vehicles bumping their way around the streets of Havana.

Wandering round Havana at night I was caught up immediately by the exoticism of the place, the warm humidity of this coastal city, the unkempt nature of the whole city that seemed to be falling into rack and ruin. Old tenement buildings like those you find in central Paris were falling into decay. Some had already been replaced by shiny new tower blocks overlooking the sea front. The sea itself slapped gently against the Malecon, the main coastal road that you see on any picture of Havana, that leads up to the old fortress that dominates the main estuary, leading into the city from the sea. How many wars this fort must have seen, how many invasions had taken place I did not know but the solid edifice looked worn by time and history.

The music and festivities went on all night and early into the morning. Stayed in friendly *casa particular* with Aussie girl (Sara) met on the plane, very cute, but on a serious comedown after spending a long weekend drinking and taking coke at various parties in London. I don't think she'd slept in days. We decided to stay together to cut cost in two. We'd found a *casa particular* near Buena Vista, it had to be done, and I am looking forward to discovering Havana properly tomorrow.

Day 2

Tropical storm at sea last night, odd sleeping patterns, 8 am and music has started already, kids in school uniforms, everyone neatly (though not expensively) dressed, nice shoes. Old and young slowly strolling to work as though there wasn't a care in the world. Every now and then a car horn tooted to a rhythm, each with its own harmony.

Breakfast: eggs, toast, fresh mango juice.

Fucking Cubans. Spent the day being ripped off today, though very elegantly, by someone who seemed to be my best friend. Henry spoke perfect French, he spent the afternoon with us (me and Sara) showing us around, translating, getting taxis, helping me out at the marina. No luck there, only three foreign boats and they were all going to America. Some Cuban boats and a lot of unidentifiable boats that had been locked down for the winter, if this is winter. Lots of security, when I went anywhere near a foreign boat a security guard came up to me, I muttered to him in English and this seemed enough to make him go away. All the boats I met were going on to the States. Apparently it is the wrong time of year to be returning to Europe.

Henry told me he could get some Cuban *pesos* instead of *pesos convertibles* but only Cubans can do this. I wanted Cuban *pesos* because Cubans buy things cheaper and it meant I could go in Cuban shops where everything would be half the price than for the tourists.

The fucker left me outside the bureau d'echange, talking to his taxi driver friend, who explained that the system was *politico*; it was, according to the taxi driver, very difficult for foreigners to get Cuban money, for political reasons. He told me he was an ex-policeman and introduced me to real policemen (with machine guns and uniform). I gave him the money and he short-changed me for £50 (which is quite a lot considering I only gave him £65 to begin with). I didn't realise at first and sat waiting for him to come back to the restaurant where we were waiting (Sarah and I that is). When eventually he didn't turn up I tried to pay for the meal with the money he'd given me and the barman wouldn't accept it because it was Cuban *pesos* not *Pesos Convertibles*. I then calculated how much it was worth and realised how much I'd been ripped off for. Shit. I hate being ripped off and would have happily paid for a meal for Henry, and even given him a bit of money had he asked for it.

Got done with false note thing as well. Or rather Sara did. Another nice Cuban offered us a coffee and introduced us to his family and asked if she could change a ten dollar note, which Sara happily did. When we got back to the CP it turned out that it was a forgery. At this rate it is going to be a very expensive stay.

Went for a meal in the evening, in an official restaurant, we didn't want to get ripped off again. So we ended being ripped off by the government instead. It seemed quite expensive by Cuban standards and I hope I can work out the currency thing so I can spend less money otherwise it is going to be a very expensive stay. The food was alright but a little bland. I had fish with the over-boiled veg that I think you get everywhere in Cuba, I suppose they want to make sure any germs are killed.

Slow walk back to the CP along the Malecon watching the young lovers sitting on the wall holding each other in their arms. I lent over the wall to see another young couple hard at it and a couple of dirty old men standing nearby. I didn't want to appear one myself so I didn't mention it to Sara and we wandered back home.

Day 3

Met Carlos and (*la Chica Mulata*) again, Carlos is a *jintanero* who lived in NY for 18 years with a wealthy wife. His punters in Havana include Jack Nicholson. He doesn't try to rip me off and has some good contacts and knows where to get the best *mojitos* in town. Yesterday he introduced me to a Swiss music producer who's interested in my rhythms in wood sculptures and wants me to perform with his band and do a video. Havana is a town of many promises and broken dreams. Anyway two *mojitos* later I was walking down the street when I bumped into a friend of Henry's. I told him I was looking for Henry (a lie) because he stole money from me (a truth). He asked me how much so I told him £600 (another lie). Hopefully this will keep Henry busy trying to explain to his friends what he did with all that money when in fact he only stole £50.

Pedrito, from the *casa particular* in Havana, gave me a lift to Cojimar. I can't give the address because Cubans are not allowed to speak to foreigners and I don't know if I'm staying here legally or not. Pedrito seems honest enough and is happy to perform his taxi service on the back of his motorbike, which is probably the best way to get around Havana.

I am now writing this in Cojimar, of *Old Man and the Sea* renown. Don't think it's changed much since Hemingway's days except that everything is more run down, with the exception of la Terraza which is the bar where H is said to have written *The Old Man and the Sea*. I think I'll go there tonight for dinner though I can't really afford it – $18 for lobster – I'll have to write something there just so I can say I have.

There are however plenty of old men going out to sea, though unfortunately there are no sailing boats any more. All offshore vessels have been banned by the Communist government. (Cubans aren't allowed on the internet either, but I am.) Many Cubans have computers hidden, like the radios of wartime France, in cupboards under beds etc . . . everything is controlled . . . check out the Cuban Customs website for what you can't take in.

Anyway, back to Cojimar. A great apartment: two bedrooms, kitchen, bathroom for $30 CUC a night, more luxury than I have known for years.

Real Cubans here, no-one shouting at you in English or French, some fucking gorgeous girls . . . The children here seem to be descended from the indigenous tribes, I hope they are descended from Arowaks rather than the Caribs. They look at my hairy chest as I walk by and start giggling; true I haven't seen many hairy chests, which is a bit of a surprise in such a Latin country, Italy and France are full of in hairy chests, as too is Spain.

Tried to go for swim but all is coral and volcanic rock. Must be a nightmare to navigate. I'd love to come sailing in these waters some day.

I'm smoking too many cigars and beginning to get ulcers in my mouth. I must set my watch to Cuban time, it still says midnight in this blazing sun. Black Cubans with dreads keep shouting something that sounds like 'Yea man' which is quite funny when you've got stoned in Brixton as often as I have (twice to be exact but each time someone said 'Yea man' (it might have been me, I don't remember).

Pedrito introduced me to some middle class Cubans (they've got a big *Casa Particular* though still only the two bedrooms allowed). Apparently Cubans don't pay tax. Though I suppose it would be difficult to pay tax when you're not paid anything anyway.

There's a *gato negro* sleeping on the balcony right next to me now, kids are playing baseball on the waste tip across the road. I think I'll go and do the same (as the cat, not the kids).

Too hot to sleep and the air conditioning makes too much noise. I always check my bed for scorpions before, and after, I get in or out of bed (strange, I don't know why I look after). This is because someone once told me of an Englishman who was bitten by a scorpion in bed in

Cuba. (Apparently it hurt, but scorpions in Cuba are not deadly.) I was also told about a tourist who was killed by a falling pig in Havana. I spent much time looking but didn't see any flying pigs. Didn't see any urban farms either, which are becoming urban myths in England at the moment, apparently someone is lecturing on urban farming in Cuba at Sussex University, I'll try and get in touch with him when I get back.

Fuck, I mustn't forget my waterproof money belt that I've dropped in the cistern of the toilet, it's got all my money in ($1,000American), a fuck lot of good that is in a country where there is a 20% commission on dollars, 10% on pounds, euros etc.

Sun seems to set at 1 am (English time). I think we're near enough to the equator for this to be the case all the time. I get ready for Hemingway's bar.

Lights just went out for five minutes, back on now though I'm changed and off to spend yet more of my meagre inheritance.

This is cool, I'm rather pleased with myself. Sitting in Hemingway's bar looking cool (for a scruffy traveller) I'm wearing a Paul Smith shirt that my wealthy aunt bought for me, though it is very wrinkled after 5 days screwed up in the bottom of my bag and I've ripped the pocket trying to push a large box of (small) Cuban cigars in it. When in Rome. White trousers, equally creased. I've had these trousers since I was 15, proud to say they still fit, though I've only been eating breakfast for the last four days and I'm breathing in. Reef shoes and a cheap Next baseball cap (bought last minute at Gatwick). This baseball cap the Cubans absolutely love, 3 people have already offered me more than it's worth. It's green cotton with embroidery on the top.

Behind me is a portrait of H himself. It looks original. Please don't let any dirty capitalist bastards come here and take it away, this country has been pillaged enough over the last few years, it belongs here. The tables look fifty years old, as Carlos said 'Cuba is a living museum'. The chairs certainly are. I admire the Cubans' ability to maintain things, especially those old American cars.

God these cigars are good. A Cuban lady said I looked like an old man, smoking cigars. I'm rather hoping that sitting here writing I may be taken for a travel writer or journalist and get some special attention, but then in Cuba where the press is controlled and people can't afford to eat out, the waiter probably doesn't even know what a travel writer is. Cubans are not allowed to travel, unless they win the lottery. That's what they call a waiting list to get to America. Carlos explained that you put your name on the waiting list and there is some sort of tombola system whereby your name is pulled from hat, or the official equivalent, then you are given a flight to America where you can go and live with your family.

Just took a closer look at H's portrait: it's signed 1935 – cool! Though next to it is a photo of a bottle of Chardonnay, this too is signed. Not so cool!

There are a lot of goats here too. I can hear them above the banter of the locals. The houses (across the road) are incredible, beat the French, Spanish or English Riviera hands down. Huge and occupied by three generations of Cuban families. Fuck, I could never afford to live somewhere like that. *Viva el comunismo, Viva la revolucion.*

I might try and blag a day out with a fisherman tomorrow. *Vaya, vaya comer una linguousta.*

On second thoughts I might just look like a wanker, sitting here writing at the table! Another second thought (a third thought?); I've been a vegetarian for twenty years and only just started eating fish for the last three years: shrimps give me the shits and I've never eaten lobster in my life. Lobsters are big shrimps: don't fancy a case of the runs in Cuba so I'll go for the fish: Dorado. That's the fish that people eat when they get shipwrecked and lost at sea in the Atlantic.

Waiter's nice, keeps telling me to drink so that he can fill my glass. Though I much prefer the Spanish way of leaving the bottle on the table and paying for the glass. I suppose that the wine I am drinking is from Catalonia (another H reference) I'm going to have to pay for each glass. Another privilege tourists have that Cubans don't.

The head waiter assures me that the picture of Hemingway is original, though he also told me he won't sell it to me (as if, where am I going to get $100,000 from?) These beautiful communists don't get the wealth they're sitting on! It's quite inspiring sitting here where the great writer once sat, puffing away on a big cigar, drinking rum, looking at all the photos of the author doing the same. I might see if I can get some deep sea fishing in too. That would be awesome. Pedrito seems to know lots of people, maybe he can pull some strings and get me on a boat with the Cubans. It seems quite difficult to meet real people here and not just those involved in the tourist trade and generally out to get as much money from you in as short a time as possible.

Fuck! the second waiter just walked by; a very big man! I think he's the biggest bloke I've ever seen in my life, he only just manages to squeeze through the double doors to the kitchen, both lengthways and in height! He must be carrying 30 plates in one hand . . . He just did it again!

My biggest disappointment in Cuba is mobile phones. I left mine at home thinking that Cubans wouldn't be stupid enough to scream into phones telling all their problems. Unfortunately Cubans love to talk! The guy on the table next to me seems to be talking to relatives in Miami, he keeps switching from Spanish to English in mid conversation. From the size of his gold bracelet I reckon he's an ex-pat on holiday to see his family. The pretty Cuban woman he is with he must have brought along from somewhere along the way.

Salsa is everywhere. Radio Cuba plays non stop salsa, even here in La Terraza. Cubans love only one thing more than talking, they love salsa. They also hate Americans; everywhere you go there are pictures of G Bush jnr with the words: *Es un Terrorista*, written underneath. Apparently the biggest space for concerts is just in front of the American Embassy, they make loads of noise for days on end, which annoys the Americans and amuses the Cubans. That about sums up Cuban politics: it is Anti American! Whatever America does is bad! I've heard the words revolution and *politico* dropped into every conversation, even a conversation about dogs! I saw a pretty girl earlier today with a tattoo of Ché G and *Hasta la Victoria Siempre* written underneath, she oozed sex and politics, as do most Cubans. That's some victory. Most Cuban women work yet they still find time for a pedicure!

Let's see if the travel journalist blag works . . .

Oh well that didn't work. Very small portion of salad. Dorado was good but vegetables were over-boiled and they gave me the bill $16 CUC. That's a lot for Cuba.

$46 CUC today and I was counting on living on $30 a day to survive for two months. I wish I could find a corrupt Cuban to buy my American dollars at the going rate (without the 20% commission).

Loads of photos of Hemingway in the back room (non-smoking). He's mainly fishing (though dressed very much like me) and seems to have landed sharks, bigger than the boat he caught them in (which beats the Old Man). Also a couple of photos of Hemingway with Castro and one of Castro kissing the portrait of Hemingway. (The portrait must be original.)

A little linguistic problem I've encountered; in French *un car* is a coach and in Cuban *un car* is a car – I realise now that I told the lady at the CP in Trinidad that I'll be coming by car. I'm getting the bus.

Day 4

Woken up at 1:53 pm English time, by cocks crowing, looked out of the window to see 100 (or thereabouts) Cuban soldiers march by, obviously doing military service. Even the Lieutenant in charge only looked in his early 20s. It looked more like an upper school outing than a military exercise, some of them were wearing baseball boots and one even had a pink flower sticking out of the end of his AK47.

Don't know what to do now. There isn't much else in Cojimar and I'm booked in here for tonight too. I'll have a cigar and think about it. Fuck it I'll brave the Cubans and go for a coffee.

Too early for the Cubans, nothing open yet, anyway I don't know if they do coffee in the bars around here. Lots of fresh fish though.

Went for a walk through the banana plantation, the sweet smell of bananas ripening reminded me of my childhood. I don't know why – this is the first time I've seen a banana plantation! The other side of the plantation were endless rows of tenement buildings stretching out for miles like a suburb of Moscow or the Spanish Riviera – except that there were vultures flying overhead.

Went to the shops. Too hot. I don't know what Cubans do but there seem to be as many hanging around as at work. I don't think they suffer from the same Proletariat work ethic that causes me to feel guilty when I'm not doing anything.

Lunch: spicy sardines with chick peas, peppers and pasta $6.60 plus a beer. Cubans could not afford to eat like this. Everyone said I could buy mangoes everywhere, so far haven't seen any. I couldn't bring myself to buy Nestlé. Had an argument with the CP lady, she wants to come in and clean, I told her not to bother, I'm only here for two days, she seemed quite insulted, suppose I'll have to trust her.

Cubans aren't as hospitable as the Spanish and it's more a case of *Mi casa es mi casa* and you're paying to stay here. Nonetheless they are as friendly if not more so than the Spanish and even if they don't offer a coffee or a beer when you go to their home they do offer water. They would probably be more generous if they had anything to give. Another thing, the couple of Cubans I've got to know who are not *Jintaneros* have refused drinks when I've offered. To this extent Cuba reminds me of Prague; the Czechs don't buy rounds. The food is also similar to food in the ex soviet countries (see what I ate yesterday). There are of course more bananas and mangoes but these aren't served in restaurants for foreigners.

The cat just got into the bin to lick the sardine tin clean. The animals here are mangy but well loved.

10 pm GMT

Just been bathing in rock pool, just me and a little clown fish. Sat watching a pelican fishing. It was a big black one, bigger than the grey ones I've seen in Costa Rica and more aerobatic than its grey cousin too, they don't dive, the grey pelican just folds its wings and plummets into the sea with a big splash. The black one displaced its wings so that it sprang nose first into the sea twisting as it hits the water: seemed to go a lot deeper.

Just met some Cubans, mulattos, that all the whites tell me not to talk to. Michel, pronounced Michelle (his dad lived in France), very talkative, seems genuine enough. Ripped me off for 3 mangoes $1, they should only be about 50 *pesos Cubanos*, that's a mark up of about 1000%. He kept me talking while his brother went off in a car. I panicked and came straight home. So far nothing. It's a shame that I have to be suspicious of everyone. They've invited me to drink with them later. I think I'll go, but not over comfortable after my bad experience. I know where he lives this time which may make a difference. Money belt in bog again though and I'll take as little as possible. I always hide my money in the toilet cistern wrapped in a waterproof pouch. Though I'll stop doing so if this gets public. Just realised that I forgot to pay Michel, must be the first time a Cuban has been ripped off by a tourist.

Phoned Mum. Woke her up: 1 am in France.

Oh no: smelly farts, constipation, burping – this forebodes bad weather on the horizon. Shouldn't have eaten that mango, it was good but slightly bitter. Don't think I'll go out tonight. Don't know how I'll come back.

TRINIDAD

Day 5

Just woke up thinking about Michel's cock. Physicality is very important over here, physical strength and muscle size are talked about and admired openly, there are lots of well-shaped bodies, both male and female. I didn't understand why M made such a fuss about showing me his cock but he must be very proud of it. He took me round the back of his house to get it out. It is probably the biggest cock I have ever seen, then I've

24

never seen a black cock before. It is almost as fat as it is long with a big floppy red head. I think it was Michel's cock that woke me up yesterday. Now I realise what the fuss was all about. I awoke today to another cock. A big strong cock is a sign of vigour and its owner is very proud, not surprisingly. I don't know if cock fighting is legal in Cuba but in the countryside and small villages it certainly goes on. In Havana I saw people training dogs, mainly Staffordshire Bull Terriers, the dogs were being made to run along the street pulling heavy weights. I think Michel wanted me to watch his cock fight. There are some things that I'm going to struggle with in Cuba; I didn't try to explain that I'm vegetarian. I don't like to eat cock and I don't like to watch them fight.

It must be very difficult for homosexual men in Cuba, a place where man to woman relationships are more important than anything except children. I know in the Caribbean in general homosexuality is not tolerated. A friend from St Lucia once told me proudly how her brothers publicly executed a gay man, they tied him to the bonnet of the jeep and drove around all the villages before taking him down to the beach and hanging him from a bendy palm tree. I don't know if homosexuality is legal in Cuba. There is a wonderful Cuban film called *Frése y Chocolate* which is about the struggle of a homosexual communist when homosexuality was a criminal (and I believe capital) offence. I certainly wouldn't like to be a gay man in Cuba. I have two friends who are a gay couple who are coming over to Cuba next year. I must ask them how they get on.

I do like the rugged simplicity of the people here, I'm sure that's what attracted H here in the first place. He probably went to cock fights himself. Though it's this superficial and material relationship with the world that will eventually put me off Cuba. It would be good to meet some educated Cubans. So far no-one has mentioned communism. I had been forewarned that politics is a taboo subject.

Slices of mango on bread for breakfast. A bit of a risk but seems alright. Mango farts a bit smelly though.

Lady from CP brought me a coffee again today. She did it yesterday. The way she gives me coffee you'd think she was selling drugs. She whispers from behind the shutters in the kitchen '*caafé, caafé*' and then slides the coffee between the bars of the window without a word and closes the shutters behind her.

Pedrito turned up on his bike and off we went for the bus. *Hasta la vista Habana, bienvenido Trinidad.*

Great journey from north to south of Cuba. Air-conditioned tourist bus 4-star luxury compared to the Cubans we passed huddled into an open top lorry. Seems to be some sort of official hitch hiking, people in uniforms were standing next to groups of hitch hikers, they flag down lorries or cars and note the number plate as people get a lift. The initiative of Cubans is astounding.

Apart from heading towards the mountains, the palm trees and banana plantations, not to mention what looks like a marijuana plantation, the scenery is much as you would expect. Rolling, bush-covered landscape, nearly 100% deforestation though. A couple of things of interest:

Went past a state prison, huge tower block surrounded by a large yard and big walls, probably big enough to house 1000 inmates. By the far wall two convicts were standing holding what looked like concrete blocks above their heads while the guards looked on. I've never seen anyone being tortured before! I hope I misunderstood what was happening but I don't think so.

The only advertising (and Warhol and Lichtenstein would love this) are huge billboards with pictures of George Bush and the words TERRORISTA underneath. Another showed Bush and equal sign then Hitler. Everywhere in Havana and little pueblos are walls covered in revolutionary messages that I can't be bothered to write down, but I'm sure all Cubans learnt them at school.

Maybe I should go down to Guantanamo to demonstrate. It seems like strange hypocrisy to have billboards showing a terrorist and then rent to the same terrorist to imprison people he considers to be terrorists, and this same terrorist claimed that Cuba was allied with other terrorists. This is probably all I'm going to say about politics, you can understand why and I'm sure I've got all this wrapped round my neck.

Got to the CP. Perido and Ilenar are extremely kind, told me 'any friend of A's is a friend of theirs'. I negotiated a price to stay here mid-week with breakfast. We chatted a bit about life and Ilenar asked if I was going to eat there. I felt very flattered and was looking forward to eating with the family.

My food was served up on the terrace while they ate in the dining room. I told them that I thought I was going to eat with them and this made Pedro laugh. It's going to take me time to get used to this. Everyone I spoke to outside the CP said not to tell the police I'd spoken to them. The people who run the CPs know what to say but won't go far in conversation. I also get the feeling they are held responsible for my behaviour, as they want to know in detail what I will be doing. I'll have to tread lightly here. Shame, I was looking forward to watching Cuban TV.

Huge dinner prawns!

They've got a parrot too.

Perido uses the polite form *usted* to speak to me but his mother says *tu*. I'll just stick to being polite to begin with. I'd brought a bottle of malt to share with my host but I don't know what to do with it now.

Had to take water from the fridge. I suppose I'll have to pay for that too. I don't believe you should be made to pay for water. I have to accept that I choose to pay for it.

I'm tired, must be jet lag, it's only 9 pm Cuban time.

Day 6

Slept well with regular visits to the loo. Got to live off £100 a week and already spent £200, be good if I can find someone to exchange my dollars (without paying well over odds in exchange rate).

Perido and Ilenar are very kind, Cuban humour is very direct: 'don't worry I won't rip you off!' P says jokingly. He also told me that his Commandant won't allow him to have a computer.

Just caught a glimpse of myself wearing my famous baseball cap and I realise why the Cubans like it so much. It looks very much like the caps the soldiers wear here yet it is embroidered on the top. This fits in well with Cuban mentality, like the soldier with a flower in his gun or photos of Ché & Fidel in the 70s that most foreigners like, or have heard of, then it is only because the look is so cool; unshaven hippies in army uniforms fighting for an ideal! It's like the old Cadillacs one sees everywhere, they are cool not only because of their style but also what that style represents: 50 years of resistance against globalisation.

Anything new in Cuba is Chinese. Perido was showing me his new air conditioning unit and fridge (new this year) both of which are made in China. All the new buses and cars are Chinese; and Cuba's first amusement park is being built by Chinese (there's even a Chinese circus there) in Mirimar near Havana.

Just been told to put my shirt on if I'm going into town because the police might arrest me if I go topless; that was a surprise!

The only grocery shops where you can buy locally produced food are in people's houses. I find it difficult just to walk into someone's house unannounced; the doors are usually open and there isn't always a bell. Most of the time someone is around but they may be in the back room.

Of the two million Cubans who live in Miami I wonder how many are shot because they pop into someone's house to buy a banana!

I don't know whether I should start arguing with Ilenor about cleaning my room. I'll give them time to get to know me before I ask her not to. It's annoying when I place my stuff exactly where I know it is; strewn all over the place, to find it neatly folded away in the drawers. Took me 20 minutes to find my trousers today, who would think of hanging trousers up in a wardrobe!

Came across my first beggars today. Up until now people have claimed that they can do something for me, no-one has just come outright and asked for money. I believe begging is illegal in Cuba. But in the black area in Trinidad, that looks like an African village, straw roofs, most people walking around shirtless(!!) and shoeless, two people just came up and asked for *pesos*. One woman explained that *pesos convertibles* is the only money of any use and she needs money for her children. I don't know how true this is and anyway she's got a ration book!

It's definitely the heat that's making me tired, I thought it was jet-lag or getting used to the food, but as soon as I turn on the air-conditioning I get my energy back.

Perido (I think that's his name) told me today that his cousin, a policeman (not surprisingly) once caught someone who had cheated a tourist the way Henry did. The robber was given 25 years in prison! He then asked if I could remember anything about Henry or if I know where the robbery took place . . . I couldn't remember anything.

Met A's brother today. Spent the afternoon together. For a farmer he's very open minded and fascinated by English culture but is put off by the weather and the individualist politics. I can only agree.

Walking around so much in this heat I'm developing varicose veins, God I hate growing old. I should have come here when I was 16 and first thought about it.

Phoned Mum using a phone card today, had to dial 119 to phone out of Cuba. I wonder if anyone was listening in.

2:10 am (Cuban Time)

Just got back from local night club. It's in a cave. Very cool. Even an underground lake. Met more of A's friends. Paid for a young lady to get in because she didn't have enough money, jokingly told her that she's going to have to dance with me now. She looked pissed off when I didn't dance with her, can't be serious, she's only 19. When I did finally dance with her my legs went all wobbly and I broke out in a sweat. I wish I'd come to Cuba when I was 19. A's brother is great; a real countryman, the way he walks swinging his arms and instep turned inwards you can tell he walks miles each day. I'm glad we didn't go far. He doesn't dance.

Cubans don't walk, they don't run, they don't jump, they don't dance, they salsa. All except A's brother that is. Any other music and they move quite awkwardly, there is a natural conformity here that is very profound and they are linked together by the same rhythm, the whole island moves to the same rhythm. I reckon it's because of all that music beating away underground.

Day 7

18:30 pm (CT)

Just got back from beach, tired and sunburnt. Feeling rather antipathetic (*antipatico*) towards my Cuban friends. I need some time alone. However their kindness and resourcefulness has surprised me again; I tore the pocket of my second shirt (in England) but thinking I was going to be surrounded by poorly clothed people, I didn't think it mattered. Most (white) Cubans are better dressed than me. I showed the damaged shirt to Ilenar she said she would look at it. They've just given me back this perfectly good shirt that they sent off to be repaired.

The Beach: the beach was good. I'm not used to doing the tourist thing, this is the first time in my life I haven't had a working holiday. Tried to find a yacht. Went to marina with A's brother, he wasn't allowed in. Spoke to Carlos about hiring a yacht 300 PC (£150) a day for up to six people (no Cubans), this includes the skipper and mate. No-one is allowed to sail alone in Cuba, all Cubans are prisoners in their own country as too are tourists once they're here; nice prison anyway. I was gutted for A's brother but at least I could point out the different yachts to him, from afar. Went to the beach as A's brother said, 'Ah perhaps one day you will come on your boat and we can go sailing'. He is a true Cuban and even if you took him away from Cuba he'd want to come back; here is his home, he's happy with his lot.

2:50 pm

$3C for a bottle of water. I'm sitting on the beach looking out to sea when I realised that the blond girl lying a few feet in front of me was Sara, from the plane over and the stay in Havana. She jumped on me joyfully and declared 'come on let's go sailing'. I couldn't resist this, but I was concerned for A's brother. We asked the guy who runs the small boats and he said it was OK but we're not allowed to go alone. What I loved the most was the big grin on the sun- and land-worn face of A's brother, as we sailed out to sea. I took one of the few photos of a Cuban because he just looked so happy, he'd never been on a sailing boat before.

Anchored off by a reef and Sarah and A's brother quickly put on snorkelling gear and slipped over the side, both obviously used to snorkelling in reefs. I stood up nobly like every good sailor, to check to see if there were any sharks in the area. I don't have a clue what sharks look like on the surface, but I couldn't see anything that could have swum out of the *Jaws* movie so I slowly placed my mask on, stuffed the snorkel in my mouth, blew a few times, struggled into the flippers and fell overboard. Now this is something a sailor is not used to doing. I nearly half drowned and quickly remembered Sarah's lasts words: 'if you feel like you're drowning, blow.' So I did. Got to the surface, ripped off my mask and splashed around like a drowning cat until I got used to the flippers. Fortunately the skipper was reclining on the deck and not taking any notice and A's brother and Sarah were off somewhere in the reef. I tried to catch up with them though I didn't see much of the reef because most of the time my eyes were half in and half out of the water; the way they are when you swim. What I did see was beautiful: many different coloured fish, amorphous coral sculptured by the underwater currents. No sharks! By the time I'd convinced myself that sharks were very unlikely I was on the boat out of breath. The skipper seemed quite surprised to see me but I just nodded and lay in the sun. 15 mins later A's brother and Sarah turned up, both quite blasé about the reef: '*No hay langousta*', and went off to check again just in case. Sarah just said it wasn't as good as the barrier reef!

Sarah and a German girl she'd hooked up with, Christina, both have tongue piercings. This fascinated A's brother. '*Es para la bita?*' he asked pointing at his tongue. '*Si, claro, es muy simpatico*', was all I was able to mutter in my broken Spanish, and nodded knowingly in a manly sort of way. My ex used to have a tongue piercing, but frankly I found it frightening and was worried about the enamel on my teeth when I was kissing her. She would take it out anyway to give me a BJ, I don't really see the point, but hopefully, and I'm sure A's brother feels the same way, I will find out one day. Meeting with Sarah and Christina later we'll go to La Couva with A's brother.

Sarah must be a typical tourist, I felt a little uncomfortable walking down the street as she sauntered along eating an ice-cream and declaring quite loudly how good it was while some locals stood in the day's heat watching her eat away a day's wages!

I'm quite sunburnt – rarely happens in England but then most of the afternoon I was in sunlight in a heat of 37°C in the shade. And a warm breeze to top that up. I didn't bring any after-sun because I didn't think I'd be stupid enough to stay out so long in the sun. I'll try sun cream instead. Brown legs and a white bum, I don't like that but I read in one of the tourist guides that topless sunbathing is illegal in Cuba so I should imagine that bottomless bathing is too! This is certainly not Brighton!

Catching up with Sarah and Christina later going to la Cuava. It's Sarah's last night and I quite fancy Christina but I don't know where we'd go for sex – if I go out someone waits up all night for me to come back in, and I'm not allowed friends, and the whole family sleeps in the room next door. I don't know if I'm going to make it for another 7 weeks.

I met another one of A's friends today, she told me that she couldn't let me in because recently she had a tourist in her house who hadn't been registered, when the one who had been registered was not in. They were just talking when the police came round and she was fined $1000C for having an unregistered tourist in her house.

I told her I'd take her out for a drink next week, she can't afford to pay for herself.

LOBSTER, tomatoes, cabbage, peppers, onions, a bowl of bean and potato soup, rice and cream caramel for dessert.

It's strange I came to the country to live like a communist and struggle alongside these people, sometimes having to survive off wild bananas or mangoes, catch my own fish etc. But I've never eaten so well and I'm waited on hand and foot.

Perido told me in his rather military fashion that my room was going to be cleaned tomorrow, this he said while he was clearing the table. I'd still rather eat with the family even if I pay.

3:30 am (CT)

Back from La Cuava: La Chica from last night completely seduced me (for my money of course but who cares) while we were waiting for an hour outside the nightclub. Sarah got in before us. I was happy to wait as the young mulata caressed me the way only a young woman does – she blew down my neck, rubbed her strong little fingers over my muscles, squeezed her tight young salsa dancing legs against mine; a conversation that is purely physical. Carlos had warned me about the *interesantas*, those girls just interested in your money, he pointed out that it doesn't matter how cold or morally sound you are, eventually you'll crack. It took me about 5 minutes of smelling her sweet young perfume and of caressing her smooth olive skin and thick Negroid hair before I would let her do whatever she wanted. I've never had a relationship with anybody before that was based on a purely physical level. Once inside the club she stayed around to dance with me a while, waiting patiently until A's brother finally asked me if I wanted to dance with her. '*Claro que si*', I replied to which she giggled almost professionally. I think the dance is called ragaton, her feet and head stood perfectly still while her hips flick back and forth so quickly and she bounces up and down. More erotic than any lap dance I've ever seen; powerful and passionate. Then we danced what the French call '*un slow*', then she said she was off to see her friends. She came back to get me to buy her a packet of cigs and I didn't see her again until the end of the evening when she hung around outside to make sure I was coming back.

I suppose it's a sort of unofficial escort system. I can only justify myself by saying I've paid for massages before, why not pay for a couple of dances and a pretty young escort. One thing is sure, as young and naïve as she looked she was certainly in charge all the time. I saw lots of Cuban girls with tourists.

Sarah got bought a drink by a young Cuban man, but he wanted a lot in exchange. I looked after her keys and money and took her home at the end of the evening. She's only 23.

About Cuban dancing. Apart from the salsa and a couple of other formal dances which all look like salsa, the main dance is to simulate vertical sex: the girl bends down in front of the guy and rubs her ass up and down in a very erotic way. I don't think the missionaries ever made it to Cuba. They call it ragaton.

Day 8

Woke up to the sting of sunburn. Feeling desires that I haven't felt for years now. It's been nearly a year since I've felt the warm caress of a loving woman. Though the swollen haemorrhoids remind me that I shouldn't try to dance through the night with 20-year-old Cubans.

Unfortunately Christina didn't turn up last night. I was going to ask her if she wanted to go to the river next weekend. Apparently it's quite beautiful and we could have shared the costs of a CP. Tourists have to stick together a lot here if they want to survive.

I'm sitting here watching the house parrot, it's a green Cuban parrot, very similar to the Amazonian parrot that my cousin has. This one seems very old and a little crazy, must be due to all these years of solitude. Every time it turns its back a hedge sparrow flies down and steals its food. The lonely old parrot looks on as its food is devoured by the other bird, it squawks and points its wing forward, not in an aggressive way, more to say hello. Its little robber friend sits on the floor eating the parrot's food, with no thought for the colourful creature, then flies off with complete disregard for the lonely old bird left on the perch. The parrot has now tipped its food tray on the floor as if to encourage the other bird back. Nothing is keeping the parrot there but on its perch it remains, rocking patiently backwards and forwards waiting for its robber friend. P just came through and asked me to give him 20 PC to buy water for the week.

When I asked A's brother if drugs were legal and told him about the marijuana plantation he looked a bit puzzled, first he said that it was probably organised by the state, then he thought about it a while before saying: 'it's not good to ask too many questions'.

The only expensive modern cars (nearly always Audis) that I have seen have red number plates, at first I thought these were hire cars but hire cars are never that good. The red plates must belong to Communist Party officials. Seen mostly by the beach at weekends. I suppose the few Cuban yachts I have seen belong to high ranking officials as well. I wonder if they own the marijuana plantations too.

I'm getting very paranoid about this diary. Perido keeps looking at it and he just asked me if I was keeping a diary. I told him it was a letter to my mother. I think I'm going to post it to her in instalments. I don't know how difficult it is to post things abroad but I have already been warned that the Customs are quite capable of confiscating a diary if they think it contains too much information.

Can't go out, it's too hot and my feet are so badly burnt that it hurts to put my shoes on. Had a date with the Chicitta at 2, it's now 3 pm. Feel a little guilty about standing her up because she can't afford to get into the night club (it opens at 2 pm on Sundays) without me. Her name begins with L. Though I'm a bit pissed off that she hasn't asked me my name yet: not very professional. Ah well she'll learn. I hope she doesn't turn into a prostitute, hopefully there is enough protection here in Cuba for muchachas like her. In other Latin American countries she'd be a cheap whore.

7:40 pm

Just had a siesta, woke up to the sound of thumping rumbla or raga or whatever it's called, and a giggling parrot. I thought it was the baby giggling at first. It's pouring down, a real tropical storm and very refreshing, I'd like to take my clothes off and stand in it. I think that's how the parrot feels.

Just had a long chat with Perido, he was telling me how he was champion of Cuba for motor X four times running until he came off and broke both arms and both legs. I suppose that's how he came to get a *casa particular*, he also knows how to toe the line.

Found out more about the Guantanamo Bay dilemma. According to the official tourist guide the Americans are here illegally and were meant to have had a treaty until 2003 in 2002. When the guide book was written, the Cubans were expecting them to leave at the end of the treaty, a source in England told me that now the Americans have a lease on Guantanamo Bay. Fidel must be turning in his grave, not that he's dead yet of course, though politically he is.

Day 9

Began Spanish lessons today with Juana. She explained to me lots of cultural things. Most importantly Cubans treat their children like children all their lives. Even a 40-year-old man will be treated like a kid. In fact they never leave home. If they do leave home it's because a house has become free in the street or at the furthest away, in a nearby village. This explains Perido's and Ilena's behaviour, they want to do everything for me. Perido even wanted to walk to school with me this morning. This is going to take a lot of getting used to for someone who looks forward to sailing on his own for days on end. They must think I'm mad. Cubans live with their parents all their lives. Usually the man moves in with the wife's family and everybody looks after the children. So far I haven't heard a cross word, lots of singing and dancing and laughing, but not one cross word or voice raised in anger. I'm beginning to feel very protective over the Cubans. God knows what will happen when the Capitalists move in! *Muerte o Patria!*

Watched the news today. Very anti America. There is a lot more footage of what is happening in Iraq than you get in England. I've seen footage of American concentration camps and the humanitarian crisis that is developing in Iraq that I have never heard about in Europe. From what I understand some guerrillas subsidised by the CIA attacked an outpost in Cuba today!

My legs still hurt from the salsa lessons. I'm going to take it easy tonight but I don't think I'm going to get much peace while I'm in Cuba.

A's brother told me today that he earns 10 Cuban *pesos* a day: there are 24 Cuban *pesos* to a pound and he still insists on buying me a drink for 40 *pesos*.

Day 10

I'm tired, legs are killing. Went out with Christopher, an English tourist. He, like many other tourists, is here before Castro dies and it all changes. Cubans seem quite oblivious to the threat of Capitalism, they probably don't mind. The whole of Cuban society is ready for a change.

A couple of builders turned up at the CP to repair the leaking roof. Perido only called them yesterday. You don't get builders that quick in England. Perido told them not to start work until I'd finished breakfast. Christopher too said he found it difficult being treated like Royalty in a Communist country. The builders are now standing on the roof talking very loudly.

I love listening to Ilenar's sing-song Spanish. I'm not sure whether she's annoyed right now but she's singing louder and quicker.

Perido told me of his son who is 29 and lives in Mexico, he had tears in his eyes as he told of how much Ilenar misses her boy.

The parrot keeps crying '*Piredo Piredo Piredo*'.

The builders are still here, they are asleep on the patio in front of my room. Quite asleep in the heat of the day. I'm getting used to keeping out of the sun. Ilenar told me to give my papers to A's brother if I want to go and visit him as he has to declare me to the police.

Today's news told about how much money the Americans and English spend on weapons. They spoke about the price of 3 nuclear submarines that Britain has recently built. It must be incredible for Cubans to hear of billions of dollars being spent. It would be interesting to know what the Cuban defence budget is. No talk about guerrilla activity in Cuba though.

Power cut today lasted ten minutes. It seems quite a normal event in Trinidad.

Sent some e-mails off today, $6 for an hour. Went out for a few beers with Christopher tonight. He's buying me lobster for dinner. I think I'm turning into a Cuban (*Jintanero*).

What chance have the Cubans got of ripping off tourists if I start doing it. Ah well, bring in a bit more money for my Cuban friends, who still charge 1 *peso* for a bottle of water! They are afraid I might get hepatitis.

Went for a walk this evening around Trinidad with Chris. How beautiful to see so many children running around in the streets laughing and giggling, playing chase. In fact there were only children, all the adults were inside watching Cuba's favourite soap opera. Every now and then a *muchacho* and his *muchacha* would appear from a concealed doorway somewhere. Cubans meet young and seem to stay together for a long time. As Chris pointed out, if you don't have to worry about work because you will always have a job and a house, all you have to think about is meeting the right girl and setting up a family. As far as I can tell mostly the man moves in with the wife's family, I haven't yet heard of any woman moving away from her family. So it is a good idea to check out your girlfriend's family.

Went to a smart bar today. The policeman on the door wouldn't let us in until he heard our accents. I don't think Cubans are allowed in.

A big room with huge open windows overlooking a badly lit square, covered in children. Very few cars around. I saw about five moving vehicles in three hours. There were lots of bats in the bar. According to Chris Cuba has the highest population of bats in the world and the most caves. He's a nature tour operator and seems very clued up on Cuba. As he pointed out tourists are probably given too much food so that the family get the leftovers. In a country where all food is rationed this is very important. It's only like my family eating food in the family hotel that had been left over from a buffet etc ... I'll try not to eat so much in future.

Day 11

Don't really know if I want to be here. Don't want to learn to salsa, it's killing my knee (I've always had a bad knee since a car accident when I was 11). I don't really want to learn Spanish, I'm only learning it because it's a condition of entry for this stupid fucking PGCE course. Certainly don't want to spend the rest of my life teaching badly behaved children in a semi state of chaos. My legs hurt, got an ugly looking rash, I'm tired and bored.

Told Perido about my knee, he just looked at me and told me to take a painkiller. Cubans are quite tough, they don't whinge in the way the French or Italians do. There are many great Cuban boxers.

Toilet attendants in Trinidad always ask for a few *pesos* before letting you in. As Chris pointed out Cuba is probably the only country in the world where being a toilet attendant is one of the best paid jobs!

Everyone drinks rainwater, it is pumped from the street into holding tanks. I can't tell if there is any filtration process, there certainly isn't any purification. I understand now why the little boy who lives in the CP where I am staying keeps asking me for water, he prefers my water to boiled rain water. I've seen water purifiers in a couple of the wealthier *Casa Particulars.*

I've had bad indigestion all day long, I don't think it's anything worse. The hot humid weather has knocked me out, I wasn't up to doing salsa lessons. Too much beer, and lobster. Chris is staying in Lily's CP around the corner, it's a lot quieter there and I'd get a door that opens onto the street so I didn't have to walk past the family and no-one has to wait up for me. If I go there it may be a little more peaceful. Though I like the family I feel awkward about joining in with them. Haven't seen A's brother for a couple of days. He may feel the same about disturbing me and Chris. I hope I'm not going to spend all my time with tourists even if that's what the government wants, I'm thinking of writing on my T-shirt: '*no soy terorista, no soy turista; soy un hombre.*'

Power cut lasted two hours tonight, A's brother turned up. He had to go home for some official papers – took him a day there and a day back, he lives 80 kms (50 miles) away! There are often power cuts because of the overhead power lines being knocked down by the frequent storms. The darkness was reassuring.

Day 12

Coco the parrot is being robbed again this morning. As Chris said, his wings are obviously clipped, which explains why he never leaves his perch.

I'm getting used to ignoring people who come up to me to offer me accommodation or food or both. The girls here seem pretty emancipated, though once they fix up with someone it's for life. I keep being told how good they are in bed and people ask if I'd like to meet girls, but as yet no-one has offered me a prostitute. Though I am also reminded every day that only Cubans with permission are allowed to speak with foreigners.

Healthwise I slept well last night. Though Ilenar has come down with flu. She might have caught it from me. I imagine that tourists bring in lots of illnesses to Cuba, which has very few major illnesses. I gave her some Nurofen and told her to go to sleep once she'd taken them, so she said she'd wait until evening before taking them.

My Spanish teacher asked if she could change my time for the lesson tomorrow because she wants to go to a tribunal at work. I was made to understand that if people have work difficulties they bring them before other colleagues to present their case. Wednesday was the day of official tribunals here in Trinidad where people come with civil cases. Today appears to be the day farmers can sell surplus stock, many houses have food for sale in the window. Ilenar has brought lots of vegetables for me. I haven't seen her shopping any other day.

The young couple who are the children of Perido and Ilenar are sitting on the rocking chair kissing and cuddling. Couples here are always in contact with each other stroking each other's hair, kissing, smiling, speaking softly with each other, like a scene out of a Gauguin picture. Couples of all ages are the same, children, teenagers, adults and even the elderly sit next to each other on the sofa or on a rocking chair, moving backwards and forwards to the same rhythm. Otherwise they are dancing together, well practised, knowing each other's steps intimately.

Earlier Chris and I with A's brother walked past a children's dance class, those thirty 9-year-olds already dance better than me, preparing themselves to meet with their dance partner for life.

A's brother keeps apologising because he can't offer me anything in return. I told him that inviting me to his house is the greatest thing he could offer. He crossed his arms in a sign of brotherhood and said

'*Amigo, mi casa es tu casa*' with such sincerity it was moving, I wish I could say the same to him but I can't afford a house in England!

4 am

Back from the Cuava. Many interesting Anglo-Cuban incidents and I've drunk far too many mojitos. A's brother fell in love with a beautiful young Indian girl from London. All the Cuban men stood around as she did a very sexy dance with a blonde English girl. A's brother spent all night trying to get a dance with her. When she started to dance with a black man he said very loudly in English to begin with then in Spanish, 'Fuck you *los lesbiennes ingles* dance with niggers rather than Cubans.' Chris and I sat there wondering if there was going to be a fight. A's brother is quite a big lad. I left him talking to the Indian lesbian and went to talk to La Chica who'd just turned up with her Cuban boyfriend. She told me she was not happy to talk right now and I left it at that, trying to drag A's brother off the three English girls who obviously wanted him to leave them alone. La Chica spent all the evening sitting opposite me. C, a friend of A's brother, asked me if I liked mulattas and slid his index and middle finger down the inside of his arm. This gesture I've seen about five times. It has more significance than any gesture I've ever come across, it means as far as I can tell; the colour of your skin doesn't wash off. I've seen black Cubans do it when talking of white Cubans and white Cubans do it when talking of black Cubans and mulattos do it when talking of the other ethnic origins. Each time it reminds me of Cuba's past and the deep-seated racism that lies in the country, that has been hampered by Communism but is still so apparent.

At the end of the evening La Chica asked me to buy her a drink and A's brother asked her what she wanted of me. Up until now she had been really friendly, but her face dropped and she said she wanted to talk to me alone. She told me that she shouldn't be talking to me because of the police. I invited her to the beach and she told me she needs $50 to pay off the police. At this point A's brother, now very drunk, barged in and asked her to be clear about what she wanted from me. She told him that anyway all I wanted was to go to bed with her (not completely untrue) so why shouldn't she get me to pay for her to get into the night club. I staggered home arm in arm with A's brother and we both declared that the English women are all lesbians and Cuban women are only interested in money. There's a definite deep male bonding growing between us!

There was a big hairy spider in the Cave. About six inches all the way across. It was just sitting in front of the toilets. I wondered if it was a tarantula and went to fetch Chris, who is a bit of a wildlife specialist. He was very disappointed to see it wasn't a tarantula. I told A's brother about it and he told me the name in Cuban – *'una grand aranee peluda'* which translates as a big hairy spider!

Day 13

Up most of the night being sick. I wasn't drunk enough for it to be the alcohol. Firstly my stomach bloated until I looked in the mid stages of pregnancy. Then I started burping, burning sensation in stomach and every time I drank a sip of water I threw up. When I saw Ilenar in the courtyard she told me not to eat or drink for 3 hours. My stomach is still bloated and burning but I don't think I'm going to be sick.

2600 *pesos convertibles* left before I break into my dollars, which I don't really want to because of the 20% commission and still looking for a passage from Jamaica to England. Not going to be able to do it though.

Ilenar reckons that the ice in the *mojitos* was made from street water and that's what caused the stomach upset. My metal crown has gone all shiny – I suppose it's the acid from the vomit.

8 pm (CT)

Just eaten rice and drunk orange juice. Seems to want to stay down. Spanish class was difficult today. I'm going to stay in and be peaceful tonight.

It's been raining on and off for 3 days now. It's almost cold: 20°C at night. The rain seems to have brought the mosquitoes. I haven't been troubled by them until now.

Three power cuts so far today. Just bumped into A's brother who gave me La Chica's address. Though not her phone number; she may not have a phone. The plot thickens. Why would she give her address if she is just *'una interesada'*? I'm quite intrigued. I might just write to her asking all the questions.

Bloody mosquitoes, I'm covered in bites, they obviously like foreign blood too!

Watched a Cuban programme called *Artes y letres*, a bit odd, three intellectuals had to ask yes or no questions about famous people. As if by magic all the famous people were Cubans, whereas the caption at the beginning of the programme includes Shakespeare, Garcia Marquez and other non-Cubans. All television is mind conditioning, Cuban TV no more than European or American TV.

Day 14

Just ate a huge breakfast, hopefully I'll be able to hold it down, though stomach isn't happy. Watching two sparrows dancing round in circles and flapping their wings, even sparrows dance in Cuba. The parrot is watching them enviously too. Sky has cleared, it's 25°C at 8 am and just a couple of clouds in the sky. I don't know whether it's my lack of Spanish or whether people are trying to confound me on purpose. Ilenar made me get up early to sign the residence paper to say I was staying another week. I suppose I should have done it last night for today in case the police came round at six this morning. The paranoia is almost palpable.

Sickness has left me very pale and wan, I now definitely look like a tourist. Hopefully I'll get in the sun today, A's brother promised to take me fishing with a *duala*, a sort of lasso with hooks on it, no rod. I hope we don't catch anything: I couldn't face having to eat semi-cooked fresh fish.

A's brother turned up to say he still had paperwork to be completed and he'd be back later. 4 pm and he's still not here, it's starting to rain so I reckon fishing is off. I hope he isn't lying to get out of fishing. I doubt it but so many Cubans have lied or misled me that I'm suspicious of everyone. Lying seems to be part of life here, it reminds me of Orwell's double talk, with such a strict government system everything exists in half-truths. I'm still nauseous and burping a lot.

Got bored of waiting for A's brother and went for a walk to La Boca, about 6 kms away. La Boca is everything Cojimar should have been. No tourists, Cubans on Saturday day off, peaceful. It's a small estuary with bush land sweeping down into the sea in front of forests rising high up to the cloud forests. I won't bore you with the details, I can only recommend that you go and see for yourself. I'll just write a list of the more surprising things I saw on my way to La Boca: a man proudly walking down the street with the biggest pig I've ever seen, on a lead. The pig was nearly as tall as most of the horses around here and bigger than the donkey we used to have. It must have weighed four times as much as well! I saw a squashed toad about a foot long, buzzards, horse-drawn taxis, beautiful wood that would have been excellent to carve, that had been chopped up for firewood, palm trees along the drives, leading to terracotta ranches, whole families, husband, wife and child on one bicycle going to the beach, fishermen rowing out to sea in wooden boats throwing nets into passing shoals. A diver with three huge pink fish (2 foot long and very fat) that he was struggling to carry down the street . . .

As I was sitting at a kiosk/bar taking it all in, two strong hands fell on my shoulders nearly knocking me off my chair and the usual cry of '*Amigo!*' resounded in my ears. In Cuba everyone is Amigo, I've never had so many friends. He asked me to buy him a drink and I told him I only had enough for the one I'd just bought (a lie of course but I didn't want to buy everyone in the village a drink). He looked surprised when he heard my accent and told me he was a Taliban. His skin was certainly dark enough and his Spanish bad enough for him to be from Afghanistan. I've heard of other Talibans living in Cuba, I presume they were offered refuge from the Americans after the first Afghan war. He proceeded to tell me that all Cubans were robbers, in front of the local policeman, who was standing in for the barman at the time, and asked me where I was from: '*soy Frances*' seemed to be the right answer and he asked me for another drink. He'd already had quite enough so I carried on with my lie '*no tengo dinero pero una otra vez*'. He sat down next to me, magicked a glass of rum from somewhere and asked me how I got to the village. I told him I walked, this he seemed very concerned about and made a gesture that I might be beaten or stabbed and told me it was very dangerous to walk home at night along the streets. I told him it didn't matter because I didn't have money or papers on me, which everyone including the policeman seemed to find funny. Then he insisted that I caught the bus, pointing at a dilapidated, run down old bus, like the one they use to pick my Gran up from the nursing home but with fewer seats and more broken windows. Apparently he was the bus driver! He said usually tourists have to pay 1 dollar (1 PC) but he liked me so I could go for free to Trinidad. I was grateful for the offer as I was going to be late for dinner at 8 pm (it must have been about 7:30) and I didn't fancy walking back 6 km up hill against the wind. 30 minutes and a few rums later a young black Cuban tapped me on the shoulder and told me to get on the bus. No sooner was I on the bus than off it went in a bang of smoke without closing the doors. Two minutes later it stopped and El Gato, as everyone called him, leapt from the bus and sat down with a group of picnickers, took a couple of swigs of rum, danced with the wife and jumped back on the bus with a fish sandwich in his hand. The black Cuban was by now trying to give me his cousin who he assured me was *muy muy guapa*, passing me a bottle of rum that he snatched from an older black man who had passed out on the wooden bench, in place of a seat, at the back of the bus. I looked at the bottle suspiciously thinking to myself 'hepatitis, typhoid, AIDS, dengue fever . . .' But as he seemed so wounded at my near refusal I took a swig. I'm sure if he'd had anything else to give me he would have done. Eventually the bus stopped at the end of my street, I don't know if that was deliberate or if that was a bus stop, El Gato had asked me which street I was staying on before I got on the bus. Nobody who got on the bus paid anything and three cyclists got on and all seemed to be dropped off near where they wanted to be. The black guy (about 18) got off and asked if I was going to La Casa de la Musica later because then he could introduce me to his cousin, banging his index fingers together again as he did before when he spoke of his cousin. I don't suppose that gesture meant I could dance with her. I told him that my fiancée (another lie) was waiting for me in *la casa particular* but he said that didn't matter he'd still introduce me to his cousin. Cubans are very persistent when it comes to sex or ripping you off, and he seemed to be organising both. Anyway I told him I might see him later. Hopefully there'll be another black out!

Day 15

The Dalai Lama once said 'if you think you are too small to make a difference try sleeping with a mosquito'. I hate people who are always right. There must have been two of the little buggers taking it in turns to whine and whirr inside my ear all night long. Didn't get much sleep, but when I did sleep I dreamt vividly I was in England with friends I haven't seen for twenty years. We were walking through town when I asked one of them what the date was. I realised it was too soon for me to be back in England and said, 'This must be a dream, I should be in Cuba right now.' I woke up in Cuba. Am I a butterfly dreaming I am in Cuba?

Church bells? I can't remember them last Sunday, but then I didn't wake up so early – 8 am. Even the bells ring to a salsa beat: *uno dos tres uno dos tres* . . .

Just killed ten mosquitoes whilst having a shower, revenge is sweet.

Went to the beach today. It rained!

One of the things I like most at the beach is watching the fishing fleet that has come out of Casilda. I'll try and go there one day and see if I can hitch a ride; it would be great to go out with these sailor fishermen. They have little 2-stroke outboards to get them going but once out of the port they put up their homemade lateen sails and sail as far as the reef. It looks so peaceful out there as they sit under canvas canopies keeping out of the sun. Some dive overboard with spear guns, others cast nets. It's hard to tell from the beach but I haven't seen any of them line fishing. I don't know if they have rods, haven't seen any in the shops. Went to the marina shop to see if I could buy a rod. Carlos at the marina said he would rent me a couple of rods or he could take me out on his big fishing boat. Sounds expensive to me.

A's brother explained the number plates to me: yellow for Cuban residents, red for rental vehicles and blue for state owned vehicles. I suppose my theory about corrupt state officials was wrong. Spoke to A on the phone – cost a lot of money: about £1.50 a minute at least. The two brothers got a quick chat. A said if I go to his family's house it is better that I pretend to be his wife's cousin, it will avoid suspicion among the other villagers.

Still burping and farting a lot – A's brother too – I think I'll just have to get used to it. Had a pizza on the beach; salty pastry probably made with seawater. At one moment sitting on the beach A's brother jumped up and said, 'what is that in the sea?' I looked and said at once: oh it's a crisp packet. Nothing unusual there, but he insisted on swimming out to sea to be sure and seemed quite happy with himself: 'look it's a crisp packet'. How wonderful that he is so unused to seeing pollution in the sea.

Just had an argument with Lilly, Ilenar's daughter, who also has a *Casa Particular*. I was joking about our night out with A's brother, she said how unfair it was that men could dance with many girls but girls are not allowed to do the same!

Watched Zorro with the family; strange to watch Zorro in English with Spanish sub titles in a Latin American country. They get most of the big American films on TV, which is a bit of a surprise too. Nearly all Cubans wear T-shirts with something English written on them, seen some strange things: The American Union of Welders, Leicester City FC and US Marines, are among many of the surprising titles to see coming down the street. I should have brought my Scarface T-shirt.

A's brother has invited me to stay for a week in July. I think going to Jamaica to look for a boat is getting less likely.

The man of the house has been away for two days now and the women have not stopped arguing, I don't know if it is cause and effect or if they're just getting used to me being here. When Cubans argue in their sing-song Spanish it sounds more like broken polyphonies.

I'm hungry. It's a pain having to wait for my meal to be cooked. I miss not having my own kitchen (galley).

Lobster for dinner tonight, see what comes up later. As the sun went down hundreds of bats took to the sky.

It rained all night.

Day 16

Five hours of Spanish lessons this morning, I think my head is going to explode. Making lots of progress and I'm learning to be rude to Cubans in the street!

4.30 pm

Just sent postcards to England and France. See whether they get there. I don't trust anyone outside the family I'm staying with. I asked the lady at the post office if they were sure to be sent as they are for my mother, she laid them on the desk and walked off waving her hands. Not very reassuring.

Had a conversation with Perido and Ilenar. They were surprised to hear I like cooking. Ilenar reckons it is because there are lots of feminists in France!

Another walk to the top of the hill behind Trinidad, the hill where the Cuava nightclub is embedded. Great view of the sea and mountains, was able to situate myself a bit better. Be great to wander up to the mountains and camp out. About 20 km to the waterfalls – could get there and back in a weekend, if I cheated and got a bus part of the way it would be easier. Wish I had a map of the area though. One might be able to see Jamaica on a clear day, saw a rainbow over an island. It's more likely to be the Cayman Islands. I must get hold of a map to find out where on earth I am.

Came back via the Cuava Hotel, at first the guard wasn't going to let me into the compound, I must be beginning to look like a Cuban, but once he heard my accent he let me in to check the prices. 60 CP a day for a room, 120 for a bungalow for two people. Self-contained with great view, food all day as far as I can tell, swimming pool and well mown lawn. This colonial residence hosted only a few French tourists and an army of security guards (about 20) most of them armed with shoulder holsters. Everything was pristine and well kept like the tourists with their shiny cameras.

Walked out of the main entrance straight back into Cuba, a shabby man was sitting next to his fat pig gently caressing its testicles with as much love as a newly wed. Another was walking up and down the centre of the street with a piglet over his shoulders shouting 'piglet for sale, piglet for sale', a half starved horse was standing staring at the tourists in their highly polished hire car who were wondering how to get past to their sanctuary on the hill. Women selling bananas, eggs, herbs and spices from various windows. Some *muchacho* trying to sell me revolutionary 3 *pesos* notes . . .

Chips for dinner!! What a treat, and potato chips not banana chips. No lobster though. I think I'll ask for lobster and chips before I leave just so I can tell people back home that I ate lobster and chips in Cuba.

A's brother's last night in Trinidad. He told me this is the best holiday he's ever had. I chuckled self contentedly for a while, then thinking back it's one of the best holidays I've had too, for many years. As we were sitting at the bar two Germans sat down and were charged 9 PC for the same drinks I'd just paid 2 PCs for. The German gave the barman a 10 PC note and told him to keep the change. Not a bad mark up if you can get away with it. The same barman has stopped smiling at me since I made him give me the right change, he tried to give me 50 PC instead of 1 CUC coin change: only 30p difference but it's the principal that matters.

Day 17

Can't believe I've already been in Cuba 17 days. I'm beginning to enjoy it. It helps that my skin has darkened. People keep shouting things at me in Cuban and they've stopped asking every 100 metres, 'What you look for, Amigo?' Now it's *'la tiendra esta cerrada, no puedes pasar!'*

Just spent last hour trying to contact yacht clubs in Jamaica. Can get into all websites but when I try to contact them the page is blocked. Looks like Jamaica is out of the window then, I'll see how much a return flight is anyway. A French teacher has contacted me about sailing *Bullet* in England. Not a transat but I'd be happy to do some sailing this year.

Looked at a map today I'm too far north to see Jamaica, apparently can be seen from the hills in Guatanamo. The Caymans are not too far from here though.

Just finished salsa lesson. Teacher is encouraging but I wouldn't want to dance with anyone else. I'm continuously hungry. A's brother reckons it's because I'm vegetarian; I need to eat meat because of the heat. In Spain I was once told to eat bull's testicles to keep up my sperm count. I think I'll stick to vegetables and fish. The hunger may also be thirst; it's too hot here to be dancing, even if it is raining again. I often think I'm hungry when in fact I'm dehydrated. The parrot's been going mad since we started dancing. It is singing and whistling.

On buying a house in Cuba:

It was explained to me today how to 'buy' a house if you are Cuban. All houses are owned by the state but belong to the person who lives in them. If a person wishes to move house they must ask for a new one, which means filling in lots of forms explaining why, if you are married, have children etc. However if your house belongs to you, you can choose who is to live there. When you die you usually leave your house to your family. However some people accept bribes to hand their house over to the interested party, of course this is completely illegal. Because it is illegal you should only accept a bribe from someone you can trust because they can always turn round and tell you they are going to keep the money, car, computer etc, whatever the bribe might be. There is nothing you can do to make them pay you back because you are already breaking the law. The best thing to do if you like your home is to hand it on to your family, who most likely live there anyway!

7:30 pm

Another tropical downpour. It's been going on for hours. I've noticed all the people I live with in the CP are coming down with colds.

I suppose I'm going to have to give up on the idea of a boat home. I'll try and get in touch with Dave see if he wants to come and spend a week in Habana.

Day 18

Keep having a recurring dream about saving people from gangsters, it started even before I got to Cuba but only once I'd decided for sure to come. I don't know much about the Cuban revolution but I know it was essentially a war of the working man against corrupt gang land bosses.

In my dream I had to save a friend by running across London, the traffic was too bad to get a taxi. I jumped into a large Bentley and told Robert Maxwell's son, who was wearing a tweed hunting suit, that my friend was going to be shot. He said he'd help and sent some armed men with me. I hid in the back of a van to get in, there was a big shoot out and I got in a fight with some skinny bloke in the checkout queue at Tesco's, but couldn't or wouldn't swing a punch. Woke up.

There's something in Cuba I feel I'm just getting in touch with. I'd like to know more about Afro-Cuban religion and the Orishas worshipped here. I've seen Lazaruses in many houses but I haven't seen any signs of worship or voodoo.

2 pm

Just met two Aussie girls, last night they had their car smashed (lights and tyres slashed) this morning some *muchachos* told them they could repair the damage for a price. Yet another tourist scam.

Went to La Casa de Musica, saw La Chicitta, we politely ignored each other, I've thrown her letter away, silly old romantic that I am.

Day 19

Cat's howling at the full moon woke me up last night. Raining all day. Went to Internet café after Spanish lessons. Power cut half way through. I'll remember only to take 30 minutes in future. Was going to go walking in the mountains this weekend but with this weather don't know what to do. Camp site number 99540231.

When it rains in Trinidad you get wet or you stop in and watch TV. When it rains and there's a power cut (most days) then you pick up your guitar or stare out of the window at the few passers by there are. I saw a humming bird yesterday!

I'm beginning to allow myself to enjoy something as puerile and meaningless as dancing, maybe I'll begin to allow myself to enjoy life.

Day 20

Still raining. Heavy downpours during the night. Nothing open because of the rain. Builders in the CP early this morning.

Roads were nearly flooded, up to a foot of rain. People take their shoes off to cross the street. By the afternoon, when the sun had come out they were dry.

I think I'm depressed. People are smiling at me everywhere but I can't force a smile back. For two weeks anybody who spoke to me who I didn't know just tried to extort money from me. I don't trust anyone. The lack of sleep doesn't help. I need to achieve something to do something for me. Bollocks.

45 minutes of salsa lessons: that didn't help much. Teacher didn't seem very happy that I told her this was my last class. She had prepared lessons for next week. We went through them all in 45 mins, fast track Cuban style as she kept saying and observed that Spanish lessons were more important than dance class. This seemed obvious to me but I found it difficult to explain. She certainly wouldn't think a tourist couldn't afford $6 a day for dance lessons. My thumbs hurt! Le cafard and that fucking parrot won't shut up!

I'm not the only one in a bad mood, everyone in the house is shouting.

6 pm

Don't know whether it's the hunger, the heat or the lack of sleep but I'm lacking energy. I'd like to do more Spanish though. I'll go and write an e-mail of complaint to the language school I came out here with, they told me I'd be having 5 hours a day plus 2–3 hours homework. I'm getting about 3 hours plus ½ hour homework. There's still lots I can do myself but that's not the point.

8.30 pm

I'm falling in love. Ah, the vicissitudes of life. Just met J. She must be a descendant of a colonial though mixed with Northern European, fair skin, turquoise eyes and walks like a ballerina. She speaks English and French and is fascinated by the outside world. Everything about her . . . just stopped to chase a frog out of my room . . . everything about her reminds me of a Spanish aristocrat, the way she holds her head and nods seriously when she agrees with you, her shoulders remaining perfectly straight. She's like wine . . . But not Cuban wine! Yet superficially she's like every other Cuban, well worn clothes, an air of being lost when she looks at the horizon. She can salsa of course and longs for independence. Looking at her slim white hands worn from manual work but still elegant, I should think she plays the piano. The way she jumps on and off her bicycle reminds me of one of those wealthy Trustafareans who are playing at being poor, the discomfort is almost amusing. Yet she

49

frowns like a Cuban, struggles to smile the way Cubans do, slightly selfconscious of her teeth, that need a bit of dental work, and speaks with a strong Cuban accent, though corrects herself when I'm having difficulty understanding. *Le coup de foudre.* Unlike most Cubans her age she doesn't wear cheap gold or cheesy American clothing. She longs to go to London so she can buy good quality clothes from a charity shop. She's heard she could buy a designer dress from Oxfam for £15!

Day 21

Rained all night, sometimes the force of the rain was so bad that it woke me up. No-one seems to have slept much last night. Don't know what I'm going to do today; suppose I'll learn some Spanish.

I'd go for a walk barefoot in the forest in the rain if it wasn't for all the dead rats, toads and dogs (not that many) that have washed up in the street.

The family I live with are getting used to me. At first I was *El Tourista Anglés* and then *El Tourista* now I'm *Yeson* (which is closest they can get to Jason) or even sometimes they call me *é*. Though I doubt I'll ever make *el* unless I marry a Cuban girl.

J told me today that before the revolution her family owned many houses in Trinidad. This doesn't surprise me.

Met a Dutch tourist. He reckons that the Cubans should give homes back that they stole from the Americans during the revolution. First pro American I've met in Cuba.

A black woman came up to me and told me all her problems. I've heard it a hundred times now – '*No es facil*'. She lives in the country, did I want a girlfriend in Cuba. I told her my girlfriend lives in England (a lie I've told so often now I'm almost believing it myself), she said that didn't matter I could still get a Cuban girlfriend. As she didn't ask me for money I gave her $1 for her two-year-old. She seemed genuine enough, though would have been ready to prostitute herself for me!

Hurricane season started this weekend and every one is talking about the 200 k/h winds that hit the area two years ago. When they talk about it they shake with fear and look afraid.

Day 22

Electric storm raged most of the night; the eye of the storm must have passed pretty close because sometimes the bed shook with the force of the thunder. It rained even harder. Didn't sleep.

Weather let up this morning so I went to the old church to look out to sea. Much of the cobbled roads had been washed away, particularly in the black suburb. It was hard trying to breathe in this humidity. When I got to the top I got the usual welcome: 'Where you from, *Amigo?*' I told him I was Cuban, he didn't like that at all and started rubbing his black forearm and saying '*No Amigo, yo soy Cubano.*' But at least he took me seriously as more than a tourist, he asked me if I was married to a Cuban girl and if I was going to live in Trinidad or La Habana. This would obviously have been a huge sacrifice and more than he would wish on anybody. I suppose what he meant is that if I'd married into a Cuban family then I would have earned my nationality.

No blue sky on the horizon though the grey mist could evaporate or could condense. I hope the weather will pick up later, I could do with some exercise.

Some people say it's going to clear up, others say it's going to rain. At home I'd check the weather report on the Internet or on navtext.

Now it's too hot! But not going to complain, will say a little prayer to my Lazarus.

The tap water is red, coloured by the soil that must have been stirred up during the storm.

Wake up to the sound of thunder. It's raining again, 2 pm. Sky is getting clearer. People keep reassuring me that this weather isn't normal for the time of the year. Tried to smoke but can't stand the taste of these strong cigarettes, though I'm quite addicted to the tang of nicotine. Is it going to stop raining? Makes me wonder what Columbus's men went through before they had their heads chopped off!

The high pitched thud of heavy falling rain hitting concrete is beginning to hurt my ears. It's been going on so long I'm sure if I was on my own I'd begin to hear voices like the long distance solo sailors who begin to hear voices in the sound of the sea as the boat splashes along.

Met two French doctors in the Internet café earlier; friendly but aloof in a very French bourgeois way. The waiters and barman in the Internet café are being very friendly, I've been in there every day since it's been raining which is more than most tourists, they shake my hand and call me *amigo* without asking for a tip.

Everyone's going stir crazy from staying in, not getting any exercise, or seeing other people. The slightest thing and there's an argument. The little one can't do anything right; he keeps getting shouted at for running, for playing in the rain, for making noise, for eating, for not eating . . .

Saw Fidel for the first time on TV. Very old man with compassionate eyes. He was meeting the General Secretary of Vietnam. Everyone in the room was very respectful, even the 3-year-old said '*Mira Fidel!*' Castro is as much respected in Cuba as the Queen in England.

Day 23

Very philosophical this morning. Still searching desperately for my need for enjoyment, not just superficial entertainment. Desperate need to smile, for human warmth, yet I'm thousands of miles from anyone I know and love, and those I know and love when I'm with them I feel a thousand miles away.

Given the slightest chance a Cuban will turn into *el jefe*. They love nothing more than bossing around subordinates, even the most hardened communist would prefer to tell someone else to do the work rather than do it themselves. Quite a few times I've heard, 'Oh I wish I could sack the cleaner, this isn't a capitalist country you know.' The only reason they can't 'sack' the cleaner is because they shouldn't have employed the cleaner in the first place. The cleaner is doing work that they are paid for by the government.

It's hot again, the sun's out. The Caribbean sing-song lilt has returned to everyone's voice and smiles are all around.

The streets are full as though the whole of Trinidad is suddenly awake after a long sleep. As I was walking down the street a butterfly, orange and black with a long tail, like a kite, flew through my heart and came out the other side.

Perido's friendliness is bordering on paternity, he obviously misses his son much. He's the only man in the house, with wife, mother-in-law and daughter to contend with most of the time.

Saw a big hairy spider (smaller than the one in Cuava) sitting on the side of the road.

Once I've eaten I'm wiped out. I don't know if it's because I'm eating only two meals a day and it's taking me a while to digest after a 12-hour interval or whether it's jet lag, heat etc . . .

Day 24

It's raining again. Ilenar had a visit by national inspectors at 7.30 am. They are calling back in three days to check her papers.

Went to see J. She asked me not to come round because her mother is afraid that the police will fine her for having a tourist in the house. If I go round in future I must take my passport so they can write me down as a visitor.

I've taken J's reticence quite badly; she was the only person I thought I could strike up a friendship with. I wonder how foreign residents get on in Cuba. There was a famous Italian who was blown up in an attack by an American backed terrorist. It's quite a famous story and I was told that there is a restaurant named after him in Havana.

Just brought a book about the Orishas. I'll try and translate, though much of it is in African.

Just been for a walk in the country. Tried to get as far as the hills but took the wrong road, don't know how, there are only three roads leaving Trinidad (to the west).

Nice to get away from the hurly-burly of the big city. Strange to step back 200 years to see a barefooted black man in torn denim dungarees working on a plantation. He and his family have probably been doing that since they were brought here by the slavers.

Here's an incomplete list of African tribes that were brought to Cuba:

Mubaké, Firé, Congoma, Tacuna, Usura, Baliatu, Ayé (which is an African cult), Ebbados, Ekiti, Agocón, Sabalá, Yesa, Ijave, Machir, Arará, Apapá.

From Nigeria: Oglin, Ondó, Oyó, Lagos, Kwara, Ulkami, Hausa, Bantú, Birongo, Mucaya, Bango, Motenbo, Mayambe, Cabinda, Mandango, Banguela, Musundi, Efuk, Ibo, Ibibio, Bricamos, Ekay and many more.

At the bottom of the hill men were filling buckets with stones that had been washed down the hill, to take back to the top of the hill to rebuild the roads that had just been washed away and so on and so on. Cuba has always been self sufficient.

Just watched Castro on the telly. It was a recording of his interview yesterday. Didn't understand much but he was comparing Cuba today with before the revolution and saying that by 2010 80% of houses will have water and public sanitary systems. Then the little boy came in and started crying which set off Mum, the Dad the Grandma and the Great Grandma, everyone shouting. The temper seemed to spread into the streets where voices were raised and children were crying.

The little boy today asked his mother if I had any teeth. Everyone thought this was amusing and I showed him my teeth. I wonder if in children's logic he thought I didn't have any teeth because I can't talk! Or at least he has never heard me try to talk in Spanish.

Saw quite a few police raids (checks) today, a big grey van pulls up outside a house and a policeman goes inside for a few minutes, then comes out again and the van moves on a few houses later. Not as frightening as the raids I've witnessed in Brighton (during the Labour Party summit) where around 20 armed police kick down the door and turn the flat upside down. But still both seem like an infringement of personal space and liberty.

Just sat down with J to give her a French lesson when this big hunk of a German, Simon, a 24-year-old surfer who's studying Afro-Caribbean culture, sat down next to her. They spent the next two hours chatting away in Spanish while I listened to them telling each other what wonderful choice of music each has and how difficult it is for Cubans to live, or go, abroad. Simon must have proposed at least three times during the conversation. Generous German that he is. He'd managed to get a European grant to study Ethnology and is based in Martinique, though he is travelling around Latin America for three months. They get on very well, intellectualising the world, solving each other's and everyone else's problems, wishing the world was better. Simon is writing a book about travelling in Cuba and Cuban culture. He's got the charming, I can stroke your knees, hand gesture of Europeans who are trying to behave like Latino. I'm meeting them tonight to go dancing, let's see if he dances like a German!

I still haven't got to the beach. I thought I was going to be sick when he looked into J's eyes and started reciting poetry in Spanish. She liked it! I should have come to Cuba when I was 23.

Simon made an interesting comparison between East Germany before the fall of the wall and Cuba, today, saying that just before the re-unification of Germany many tourists brought money into East Germany and all the East Germans wanted to meet foreigners to learn about their culture and to get married!

Went out with the two lovers this evening. Had to sit there listening to them boosting each others ego, flicking from one language to another and giggling at each other's mistakes, bouncing facts and figures off each other as if to show how clever they are. All I know is that there are plenty of clever people in the world but this doesn't seem to have made the world a better place. Simon waffled on for hours with the romantic fervour of a 23-year-old who's just discovered the outside world and wants to put all wrongs right. J turned to me wide-eyed and said how nice it was to talk with someone so impassioned with life, so willing to do so much to change the world. I just told her that I was like that when I was 23 and now I've changed a lot and the world is still the same.

Day 25

La Chicitta was there with her boyfriend but she sat staring at me all night. Very flattering, I think!

Spanish class. It's frustrating I understand most things when they're said in Spanish and not in Cuban.

Went to Internet café, very slow, five minutes to open a page! At $6 an hour that's quite pricey. Nobody seems to be receiving mails correctly and my mother doesn't seem to understand the ones she gets. I asked her to pass a message onto Dave and she gives it to someone else.

Had my first encounter with Cuban bureaucracy today. I had to get my visa extended: went to Immigrations (2 km walk) where I was told to get stamp from bank for $25. Another 4 km there and back. When I got back the same official who served me before told me that he couldn't deal with me now because I had to wait for *El Jefe*. I waited for two hours, while the official served many Cubans and I watched a gecko walking on the ceiling. It then stood on a window changing colour, thinking about turning red then back to pea green and suddenly it's head turned turquoise blue; I thought it was going to be sick. Half an hour later it was green again. Then the *Jefe* walked in, a 15-year-old boy in army uniform with lots of stripes on his arm. He swanned into the waiting room, looked at me suspiciously, went into the back room and the office opened. Another man I had never seen before, much older with fewer stripes, asked me to come into the office, filled in a form that I could have done myself, then struggled to read the date of the stamp on my visa, so I told him it was the 15th May and he extended my visa to the 15th July.

So far a frustrating day. Will have another go at Internet but no news from Dave wanting to come so I'll have to find something else to do, might go to Guantanamo and start a war!

(Perido just told me, secretly, that there is likely to be an inspection soon and if asked by the police I must not tell them that I have eaten fish or lobster. Which of course I hadn't. In Cuba you can only buy these in state owned restaurants, anybody who catches fish must sell it to the state at a low price. The state in turn will sell it on.)

Now my Spanish is improving I'm beginning to open up and I'm finding the Cubans a lot more friendly. Speech is so important here: people talk constantly, mostly about nothing of interest, the important thing is to be heard. I often hear Cubans walking down the street alone talking, not to themselves, but to anyone who cares to listen. For a Cuban anyone who does not talk does not fully exist. Tourists who don't talk, who just walk around with glib grins on their faces, remind me of African fetishes, they are not really alive.

Day 26

Wake up feeling quite Chango. Surprising religion – the Orishas are bit like Celtic earth gods or fairy lore, the difference being they were all given Catholic names. For example: Oggúa, god of minerals and science became Saint Peter and Saint John the Baptist under Catholicism. Babalú Ayé, Orisha of the ill and needy became Saint Lazarus. This is symptomatic of the way Cubans assimilate other cultures and all the Orishas have a Cuban slant, some being good at looking after tobacco. Elegguá, and Saint Anthony, protect travellers and roads: very important here in Cuba where there is so little public transport. Voodoo and Catholicism go hand in hand quite happily in this country where all religions are tolerated and considered equal!

Just went for a two hour walk to the Parqueo del Cubana. Followed a footpath through tropical forest by the side of the river. Interesting to think that this footpath was probably made by Cortez's men 500 years ago just before they left, from this spot, in 1512 to conquer Mexico.

Was quite vigilant, or rather excited, by the thought that I might come across a croc. Sometimes they wander away from the swamps or are released into this river. Though the only frightening thing I saw was a 5 ft snake that looked as frightened of me as I was of it. We stood or rather we slithered (if you can slither without moving) looking at each other for a while until I carried on my walk. When it started to rain I cut down a big leaf and stuck a stick through it to make an umbrella. Though I instantly threw it away when I heard a car coming. Cubans would probably think that a tourist carrying a leaf over his head, trying to be like an indigenous, looks like a real tosser. But the car was carrying a couple of lost tourists anyway.

Legs hurt now from so much walking and I'm starving. However I find that walking is the best thing to get rid of hunger pangs.

Just watched Cuba vs Serbia in World Championship volleyball. Strange to see stars and stripes suspended next to a huge portrait of Ché. Hopefully this is a sign of things to come. With two million Cubans living in Miami most Cubans must have some friends or family in the USA, and they must like the country even if the Cuban government doesn't, and vice versa. Strange politics where Cuba sides up with North Vietnam and China as allies but everyone plays volleyball together. It's a bit like classroom politics where little Johnny makes friends with big Jack who is bigger than Sam etc . . . One thing the commentator said was that all the Serbian players are professional players and are paid to play in Italy or Serbia. The Cuban players however, are still not paid, they are playing for an ideal, as the Serbians would have done when Yugoslavia was a communist country! Le plus ça change . . .

Couldn't help thinking that the Serbian team wasn't trying very hard, they seemed to let a lot of goals go and the only way they were winning was because the Cuban team gave away so many penalties. In this world of lies, double talk and deception the truth becomes confused.

Tried to explain to Carlos (the contact from the language school) during a conversation about the differences between Cuba, France and England, why in England it isn't safe for children to play in the streets on their own. He could understand about cars and that we in Europe can't let children play freely on the streets, but he couldn't understand why anyone would want to hurt children. I didn't take the matter any further, only to say that I think it is far better to be a child in Cuba than it is England.

Day 27

Papa Chango was screwing with my dreams all night long. It's hot. Wanna go to the beach, wanna stay in bed, wanna meet Cubanas, wanna have the courage to dance.

Gracias, gracias gracias Papa Chango! I've just spent the whole day naked on a golden sanded beach miles from anywhere with a beautiful Danish girl!! *Gracias* Papa Chango, I owe you a sacrifice.

Met Christina as I was walking to the part of the beach you are not meant to go to because it's reported to be dangerous. Thought I'd introduce myself as we were the only two people on the beach for miles and she happened to be fucking gorgeous. Also turns out we have quite a lot in common, or at least I like to think so, anyway huge coincidence that we should be on the secluded beach at the same time. And both of us had cycled there. The first time I've ever hired a bicycle.

Standing by the beach watching a school of swordfish, each about a foot long, when all of a sudden I saw it. The flash of the small white triangle, the dorsal fin of a small shark. I feel like a man now. Beautiful naked young woman next to me in the blazing sun, sharks and sword fish. Saw a ray in the sea and lots of crabs on the road at night on the way back.

Met some Cubans, two couples on the beach on the way back. It is so much easier to meet people when you've got a beautiful woman with you. They were friendly and kept saying we're not interested in your money. One of them invited me fishing though I told him I was worried that he might get into trouble with the police. He said it didn't matter and we arranged to meet next week. Buy him a few drinks and we can go fishing. He seemed to know a lot about France and said he knew how difficult it is for blacks in France.

I'm taking the Danish girl (Christina) to La Cuava later, she said she wants to dance with me, just cycled 40 kilometres and now I'm going dancing all night with a 20-year-old. Should have come to Cuba when I was 23.

Eight hours later. God that was a stupid idea, fancy taking a beautiful young woman to a room full of Cuban men. The lights went out, general power cut. At one point the Danish girl disappeared during a *coup monté* where a friend (*el muchacho*) introduced me to some of his friends while another friend took her into a back room (or a back cave as the case might be) and tried to kiss her. I didn't know whether she wanted to be kissed or not so I went to find out and she told me she didn't want to go home without me. It's amazing the effort a Cuban will go to have sex with someone they don't know. While I was walking her home the two friends tried another *coup monté* by fixing me up with a pretty black girl who wanted to take me to a club until 6 in the morning. All I wanted to do was to make sure the Danish girl got home (she didn't even know where she lived). Finally I pushed the Cuban woman away (a bit rudely I felt but she seemed fine with it) then took the Danish girl home, once she'd pushed away the enamoured Cuban guy, who shook my hand and said goodbye to me gracefully and told me to call when I wanted to go out, and off he plodded to his wife and child. I took the Danish girl home and we were both surprised about the forwardness of Cubans. She asked me why I didn't go off with the Cuban girl. I felt like saying 'because I'm not a fucking animal', but thought this was a bit harsh on Cubans who in general I quite like.

In France *macho* is an insult. In Cuba it is a compliment. In the Club a woman friend who's been living in Cuba for six months agreed with me that Europeans aren't macho enough to dance the salsa.

I think the difference between macho societies and French/romantic ones is that *machismos* are strong powerful, dominating, sexy, allowing the woman to express her femininity. Though *machos* seem to need continuous reassurance by going with many women. In France a man who sleeps around is known as a *mal-baisé* and it's considered that his wife isn't doing sufficient to keep him at home. The same goes for a woman. When I am with a woman I know that she won't find a better lover elsewhere (or she wouldn't be with me) and I don't feel the need to find someone else if I'm happy with the woman I love.

J, who happens to be the most intelligent Cuban I've met here in Trinidad, said something stupid to me. When Eric and Christina had gone off together J said, 'Ah, your *muchacha* and Eric have gone off to have sex.' Although I thought this highly unlikely as Christina had told me earlier on that day that she wasn't looking for a boyfriend, I still felt I'd been robbed of something that wasn't mine. Strange emotions and feelings that I haven't felt since I was a teenager seem to be swelling within me.

Day 28

God my legs ache, my back aches and I'm trying not to think about the piles. Sunburn isn't too bad though. What a mug! Yet another day naked on the beach with C. I like a girl who openly flaunts her beauty and has no qualms about it, but it's quite tough for her here in Cuba. In La Cuava again last night another Cuban towered over her, when I was not looking, and kissed her. She wasn't very happy. On the way home a man started to follow us and was wanking. When I told him I was going to phone the police he just shrugged his shoulders and carried on. C was quite upset – it's the second time this has happened to her at night. In Havana someone did the same thing. I don't know how Cuban girls would react to this. I'll find out. But if I got into a fight with every randy Cuban I'd spend a lot of time fighting.

I've got into some sort of macho one-upmanship with Carlos (an 18-year-old Cuban), a bit silly but quite fun. Ever since I've been going around with C. he keeps asking if I've had good sex with her, I keep calling him a girl, I can't help myself and he is going to give me salsa lessons but only if I do the girl's steps. I don't know if that matters, I don't really care. I'm smoking far too much.

After Spanish class I was introduced to another Spanish student (an English girl). Very pleasant but I don't want to spend all my time showing her around. I took her round Trinidad. It took us an hour to see everything there is to see then we sat on the park bench and she asked what else there is to do. I told her nothing. She looked very surprised and asked me to take her out in the evening, I'm not a fucking tourist guide. I want to spend time with my Cuban friends who I'm just getting to know. She is welcome to come along but they are already taking a risk spending so much time with me alone, and I've got brown skin. She ought to get a Cuban boyfriend!

Spent the evening listening to C talking about herself. She's a bright girl and quite clairvoyant, though she refuses to admit it. Her mother is a mystic healer etc, sounds as though she's from gypsy descent. C is extremely cute; continuously flirting with her eyes and telling me how good she is at sex. She told me J went to see her to find out if we were fucking. Funny – I'm obviously fitting into Trinidadian society if the locals want to know the gossip on me.

5 am

Can't sleep. My ankles are itching so much. They are covered in fleabites from the beach. The fleabites itch more than the mosquitoes. No water left and I'm thirsty. I'm going to have another cigarette!

Just been outside for a fag. I can't remember when I last saw the stars so clearly. Saw a few satellites drifting through the night sky, the Milky Way is very clear. Venus is sitting coquettishly on the Little Bear and as I was staring at her a shooting star flew past. I wished to kiss C. Silly old romantic I am.

Day 29

Spanish lessons, I'm making some progress but not enough!

Checked e-mails, went a lot quicker today. Dave says he might want to come over in July. Mum is well and sister is funny. Can't stop thinking about Christina and being 22. I was in love with a woman my age now when I was 19 then but she seemed so old and was completely infatuated with me. Swings and roundabouts. Read a beautiful Cuban short story about the death of a poor woman before the Revolution. It reminded me what the political system here is all about. The family are watching *Jaws III* on telly, I think I'll give it a miss.

God I feel like killing someone. One of those days of heavy weather and lethargy, I'm hungry but can't be bothered to walk. Reading a few official school textbooks for teaching Spanish. Very interesting – every example for grammatical exercises is given in the form of a revolutionary statement, e.g. 'the fight with . . . ended in a final victory', the right answer being 'America' of course. The whole book is like it.

The thing I dislike the most about Cubans is their capacity for lying. They have absolutely no qualms about lying. When I was telling my friends about not wanting to hang around with the English girl they all told me to make up some story, pretend I was busy, was going away etc. Strange, I could quite simply say that I'll go around with her when I can.

I believe that this comes from being taught to say things they don't believe in at school.

The famous Cuban drink 'Cuba Libre' (rum and coke and something else) is popularly called *una mentirosa* = a lie.

The problem when you hang around with 20-year-old girls is that they remind you how good things used to be. I've just been told that I must have been really good looking when I had hair! I think I'll find older women to hang out with now.

Went to the Escalinatar with J and Christina.

They told me that on the beach a man came and started wanking next to them. It just seems an accepted thing here. This is obviously why Cuban girls don't go topless. Christina reckons it's ok but I still believe it is illegal (to go topless that is); pornography is illegal in this country.

Met B, a friend of J's. It was refreshing to meet an intelligent, open Cuban. He told me all about orishas and showed me his black and red coral necklace, which is the colour of Elegguá; the orisha that protects travellers. There are eight of them that correspond to the eight days of the week (?) Hopefully we'll meet again, it makes a change to talking about dancing and women.

Day 30

Back from the beach where I spent the afternoon with J and Christina. Swimming, yoga, chilling out, enjoying Christina's energy and pure sincere enthusiasm for life, stopping to stroke palm trees, laughing with the clouds, smiling at the boys, flirting with the whole world and mother nature herself. It started to rain. J fell asleep under a palm tree and Christina carried on playing hakisaki. I lay down on a sun lounger, pulled a rubber camping mat over me and lay there watching this beautiful young woman and the white beach the palms and setting sun over the azure sea. Christina turned to me and said I looked like I was sick. I was reminded so much of the closing scene of Thomas Mann's *Death in Venice*. Then it dawned on me, like the lightning that was flashing into the sea, like the pure white waves that were breaking on the reef, on the horizon, it all seemed so clear: I'm having my mid-life crisis.

Fighting so hard to hang onto to my youth, to the dreams and ambitions, the love, the passion, the strife, the fun, the fun.

For so long now I've forgotten how to have fun. Not for any reason, just to be free, like Christie; like the handsome young Cubans in the night club. Just have fun!

I think I'm having a nervous breakdown. The tears are streaming from my eyes as I write, I can hardly hold them back. I'm sitting here, crying like a baby but don't know why. Just let go, let go of all the beauty of youth, just let it go and move on. But I don't want to, I want to be Christina, I want to be Sarah or La Chicitta.

It must seem so obvious to those I'm close to, to Tess who I tried to love in vain, to my mother, to my sisters and my cousin. I'm never going to be young again, and the sheer thought of it is killing something inside.

It began on Sunday as I was lying on the beach, I dosed off for a few minutes and when I woke up one little tear was sitting on my cheek. I don't want to be some sad old man.

I want to be the care-free, handsome young man I once was, the sort that Christina would have died for, the way she describes the young men she fancies. I want to make love for hours in the Caribbean Sea, with a stranger I'll never see again, really live, feel life pouring through my veins and beating in my heart.

Power cut, the lights have gone out I've just cried myself to sleep, which I haven't done since I was six years old. Wake up to the sound of Ilenar shouting at the kid in the house.

My mind is running wild with fantasy, my heart is split asunder, it feels as though I'm bleeding within, every time I think of Christina, of her beauty and what she represents. How I wish to seduce her but know it's so unreasonable. What would a beautiful young woman see in me? I don't know when I last felt this alive ... I can't remember being so infatuated with one person so much before. This infatuation is obscene; beyond all common sense or understanding. I close my eyes to see her, I try to read and I hear her voice and I smell her scent everywhere.

When I stop to breath and think, I realise that this is what it's all about, this never ending renewal of relationships. When I say goodbye to Christina tonight I will never see her again and I know, beyond a doubt now, that she will take my youth with her. God I want her to stay and make love to me!

I've got chronic diarrhoea, I wonder if that is why I'm floundering emotionally, is the diarrhoea psychosomatic? It was hard to listen to Christina talk about her most recent sexual conquests, especially as I had to run to the toilet every ten minutes. Took a pill – seems to be working.

God how difficult and painful it was to kiss my youth goodbye. She said she'd like to meet up in Paris, but I don't believe a word of it. 20-year-old travellers believe their own promises but life rarely lets them keep them. I'm sad but not profoundly so. For the first time I looked in the mirror and saw a man, not a boy who needs his looks to get by, but a man. I hope the clouds will eventually move to reveal something new, something more open and joyful in my heart. Farewell Mariposa.

Day 31

I feel emotionally and physically drained. Maybe I should have given the sacrifice to Papa Chango. I don't have the physical strength to do anything, nor the emotional will. Yet I'm becoming vaguely aware of the possibility of change. It is as though I'm becoming aware of an uncut diamond in my soul or a small rainbow is just beginning to form in my heart and I need to work on shaping the diamond and giving the rainbow space to grow ... Stop to go to the toilet ... But the responsibility of the diamond and the rainbow seem so great. I want someone else to be responsible for my happiness but I know this can't be.

I'm not going to have breakfast today. I feel pangs in my stomach and in my heart I'm fighting to hold back the diarrhoea and the tears.

I wish I could get the image of that beautiful young woman standing naked in front of me, as she changed to go out last night, out of my mind.

Got back from Spanish class and the whole street seems to know about my diarrhoea, the uncle and father are arguing about whether I should drink orange juice or tea (I've got both now) the gran and mother made the tea. At least this way my pained love-sick expression will be misread as physical pain.

I've just looked in the bathroom mirror and I seem to have many more grey hairs.

There was a grey, tempestuous, windy storm this morning as though Oyá was empathising with my own inner turmoil. Horizontal rain and cold winds made the Cubans run for cover saying I hope it doesn't get worse, and they know how bad tempered Oyá can get.

I went to try and buy a Santaria necklace of red and black coral from one of the artisan stores. I could do with a bit of protection from Eleggúa.

The nearest I could find was a ceramic one, the lady at the stall said she would try and find me a real one, that her uncle is a Santaria. I'll go back on Sunday to see if she has found one.

This obsession for Christina is getting ridiculous. I keep thinking of ways of contacting her or of getting her to Paris, try and seduce her with presents, with love, with flowers and poems. Yet all these gifts I know I need to give to myself. If Christina represents my youth and it is my youth I long for I need to let it live in my heart, buy myself presents, treat myself . . . love myself. Though I might buy her that painting she liked and post it to her when I get back to England. Let's see if she's e-mailed me, for she showed an interest in me when she was here. She even showed me her diary entry about me: 'met this nice French bloke called Jason.' The previous Frenchman she wrote about had five pages dedicated to him.

I suppose it's the boredom that's getting to me. Now I'm feeling better.

I'm thinking of getting a tattoo, I used to laugh at those middle-aged men who buy a Harley Davidson and ride around with a young woman on the back. I always thought they look so sad, now I'm one!

Just saw Carlos (the 18-year-old *muchacho*) who apologised for not giving me salsa lessons on Tuesday but he was fucking somebody's wife! He invited me to a party tonight. It would be cool to go to a Cuban party though not if I've got to go to the loo every five minutes. I think hanging around with Christina gave me street cred amongst the young Cubans. I'm not going to tell them I've been crying like a baby since she left.

I must have been holding in the tears all my life. So many years of being tough – kick boxing, sailing, being a mean teacher (not always)!

Just holding it in, never accepting my grief except on rare occasions with Tess.

On second thoughts I'll give the party a miss, I don't think downing half a bottle of rum is a good idea right now. I should have come to Cuba when I was 26.

Just watched the news. It's Ché's birthday today and there was an interview with the man who travelled across Latin America with him on the famous motorbike. This is the real reason I came to Cuba in the first place: to see how an ideal is upheld in the long run, to witness the Revolution while it's still going on. Yet here I find myself with my own revolution, my own struggles for life and ideals, which seem so insignificant compared to the fight and death of Ché and the continued struggle of Fidel! Perhaps if we all looked at our internal conflicts and struggled to resolve them, however painful this may be, perhaps then we wouldn't need to struggle against others, we could fall in love with ourselves and not compare ourselves to others. This is the only revolution: to connect with ourselves and therefore with those around us. A man can't kill another man if his heart is filled with love. My struggle is a struggle for peace, for peace within, for peace here and now whenever that now may be, and wherever I may be.

It's cold – 20°C – the coldest it's been since I arrived in Cuba. Think I'll go to bed, hopefully there won't be too many mossies; mosquitoes don't like the cold.

Day 32

I've been in love before, but always with real women. This is an obsession with an idea, with a fantasy. I never really understood people who are fascinated by film stars or famous people to the point of becoming obsessed. What is the point of falling in love with someone you will never see again. Even the thought of never seeing Christina again brings tears to my eyes.

It's raining outside. It seems to have rained more in Trinidad than sun-shined. The sunniest days were when Christina was here.

In Cuba sixth-formers have to go and spend a month working on the coffee plantations. I think all students should be made to work for their country, to do something useful for the environment and develop respect for the place they live and feel useful themselves.

Good news – Dave is coming over on the 4th July. We will probably behave like 20-year-olds for a week. This'll take my mind off my self pity.

Though already I'm feeling lighter in my heart. And the diarrhoea is over. It's good to eat again. Though I'm cautious about what I eat.

It's been raining all day.

Yvette, the English student, told me that the Spanish lessons too are illegal. In Habana the police raided the school she was learning in and she had to hide her books. This double society is so confusing and means you have to think every thought twice, once officially and once based on what you want to do.

Electricity is flicking on and off in this weather, it's raining heavily again.

As soon as I stop doing things my mind wanders back to Christina. I'm trying to focus the same thoughts on myself, give myself presents and love!

The parrot just let out a loud squawk and fell off its perch!

Rainy days of boredom and longing; I think living with strangers is difficult, for them and for me. I feel as though I should be doing something. I also need some exercise.

I'm reading an abridged version of *The Old Man and the Sea* (*El Viejo y el Mar*), very appropriate reading. Though as yet I don't have the strength to fight the sharks, but I know they're getting closer.

Now Christina is slowly turning into a happy memory, Christina being synonymous with my youth, which I realise one day I will look back on joyfully, rather than longingly, at the happy times I had. Then I will not regret those days gone by or resent my ageing body, but will feel the memories with warmth and be content with all that I have.

I can sit here and read about the old man and his old fish knowing that they are the magnificent creatures of the sea and only age can bring this magnificence , it's a beauty that I am barely beginning to understand.

Can't sleep. Every time I close my eyes I see a vision of Christina's face as though the image is scratched into my mind's eye the way the sun does if you look at it directly. Her soft juicy lips, her swarthy Mediterranean skin (her father is Spanish) and those sensuous brown eyes enrobed in flirtatiously long eyelashes. Her young pure white teeth like those of a child, shining out from that happy carefree smile that just makes you melt into the ground. Maybe I'll be able to exorcise her if I write about her enough. I can only love her voice too, her cute Danish accent and innocent expressions of a teenager – everything to her is so 'old school', even me I should imagine!

Day 33

Went to get the steam train that does a tourist trip to the old plantations. Got to the station with Yvette and there was no train. When we asked why there was no train we were sent to see the driver. He and the first mechanic have been driving (or not) this train for 43 years. The train was built in Cuba in 1927. It's an oil heated steam train, interesting to see though black with soot and oil grime and looked as though it was going to fall apart any minute now. Apparently it went out yesterday! Once they'd showed us around they, of course, asked for money '*para una cerveza*'. Yvette is a lot tougher than I am, she has travelled in Africa, and told them no! I said we'd give them a present next time we come for a ride. The old and younger man (who'd been the mechanic for five years) looked so forlorn, not insulted, just sad like a puppy that's just had it's nose slapped for peeing on the carpet.

Yvette's really good at bartering and refuses to pay anything but local rates even if it means bartering for five minutes over the price of a banana to save the equivalent of 2p.

I had a go at bartering yesterday. I found an Orisha shop. It was in someone's front room and through the bars that cover the windows you could buy, herbs, medicines, sticks, jewellery and most paraphernalia to be blessed by the Gods or cure sickness. There were eight different sorts of necklaces for the eight Orishas. I want a real necklace, for Elegguá: red and black. I asked how much they were and was told 2 CUC each. This seemed expensive so I asked for four chains for 5 CUC, thinking that this would be a good base for bartering. The woman just shook her head and walked away. I think I have a lot to learn about trade and barter. I'm going to ask a Cuban friend to find out the 'real' price.

Whilst walking around got the usual 'where u frome, *amigo*?' from a woman trying to sell something so I shouted loudly, so everyone could hear, '*estoy de la Luna*' (I'm from the moon). This made her shout and mumble something incomprehensible and brought a smile to the faces of some nearby workmen.

I've spent £800 since I've been in Cuba (1 month) and I've just £200 and $900 left which equals about the same. £200 = 354 CUC $900 is about 900 CUC (if I don't have to pay the 20% I was threatened with) £800 – 1480 CUC and I've got about 1260 CUC to last me until 12 July. Today is the 16th June. From the 1260 I have to deduct two weeks rent 280, this leaves 880, I have the bus to A's brothers about 50 CUC return, the bus to Havana 25 CUC and air tax 25 CUC plus taxi to airport 25 CUC. This leaves 755 CUC, 20 a week on water = 80 CUC. If I'm careful, for the next two weeks here in Trinidad I shouldn't need to spend more than 50 a week – I don't forget it costs 12 to go to the beach. This leaves 575 CUC. Hopefully I won't spend more than 50 CUC at A's brother's. So when Dave gets here I hope to have 500 CUC left for eight days. Dave will have money so I'll pay him back if need be and I will be able to afford presents. Internet 12 CUC a week. I'll have to be careful with outings. Yvette wants to go to la Cuava tonight, I suppose I don't have to drink.

Just went for a walk out into the suburbs to the east of Trinidad. Not far but within minutes I was in the slums surrounded by barefoot, topless *muchachos*, horsemen, listening to the horses neighing in the banana plantations and the music, of course, the music. Every rundown concrete bunker and wooden shack trembled to the sound of music: salsa, traditional country, ragaton, classical opera . . .! Yes from a few of the waterless, open sewaged, windowless houses, Tosca, or what sounded like Tosca in Spanish was blaring out! I'll always remember the Cubans for their music, their sensitive ears and rhythmical movements. Cubans love to sing, when they are not talking they sing traditional Spanish songs with their beautiful Caribbean lilt that is so enchanting.

Somewhere someone was roasting a pig. The smell of pork scratchings and open sewers was almost intoxicating.

I tried to pick some mangoes but they were all too hard.

All the time sitting on top of the city like an inaccessible palace could be seen the expensive hotel; La Cuava (named after the cave where the nightclub could be found), with its guards, drives as smooth as marble and its neatly shaven lawns like a costly whore's pubice.

It was good to walk on my own, away from hyperactive tourists who always need a destination, a sense of direction and who fill my heart with fear. This was the Cuba I came to see. I came to meet these people, play dominoes and drink dodgy punch. I didn't come to meet Christina but I did meet her and I met her for a reason. In spite of all the overwhelming beauty of my walk I couldn't help thinking how nice it would be to take Christina and J to see the Eiffel Tower.

I always feel a lot safer in the slums than in the towns. As I walk along most people don't take any notice of me or they furtively drop a quick 'Hola' if our eyes meet. I think I'm beginning to look more and more like a Cuban now, someone said so the other night. My skin's darker and my clothes are a bit shabby and my stomach aches continuously which means I'm wearing the same discomforted look on my face. I'm even being treated like a local, the other night I was leaning with my back against the bar, sheltering from the rain when the barman came and told me to take my foot off the wall. There is no way he would have said that to a tourist.

3 am

Back from La Cuava. Nothing like dancing in a cave full of a few hundred young Cubans to raise your spirits. Saw La Chicitta. She looks so very young now I am seeing with my new eyes. How I could have thought she would fancy me I don't know. At first I was paranoid about my age then I just got dancing and everything moved. Met a couple of French guys from Lyon. They love Trinidad. I missed dancing with Christina, dancing so, so close. But then she danced close with everyone, and I get the impression that a couple of the Cuban girls moved away from me when I got close to them, but then maybe I'm getting paranoid about my age. Some really good tunes, one is just sex with a ragaton (I think) beat. *El Muchacho* was being handsome, dancing well and kissing all the girls. He asked me how many children I had. It is to be expected that a man twice his age should have kids. He showed me a few moves and I impressed myself if no-one else!

Day 34

Today I feel beautiful! So what if 22-year-old girls no longer fall in love with me and 18-year-old *muchachos* think I should have a wife and kids. So what if back home I should have a house and a car and traipse to work everyday, killing myself doing a job that my heart isn't into. All these things I can appreciate because I've done them and I've stood by myself and said NO! This is not my life. My life is here and now and it's in Cuba. Who knows what else life may bring. I'll never have time to do everything, but what I have done so far has been marvellous. And now what I do takes on such a profound aspect that every day is a personal revolution, an ideal fulfilled. Every step I take is a step forward towards me, towards my life and my love and people want to share that road with me, because it's a beautiful path I follow! It's a solid path that I walk down with the certainty of many years of experience.

I feel as though I'm growing stronger every day. Stronger than I've ever been. Though no longer do I feel invincible. I'm not going to run 18 kms to the beach because my heart couldn't cope with it! Nor am I going to lust after 20-year-old women. For the same reason.

The sun's shining, it's a beautiful day and I'm going to one of the best beaches in the world.

Got to the beach.

Walked down the long, white sandy peninsula for about 2 km, lots of butterflies, yellow, green, blue, black and red were flying up from the bushes on the landward side. Sat down on my rubber mat and towel, no-one around for miles, stripped off and lay back enjoying the peace and the sun. In the distance the fishermen were trying to sail up and down the reef but what wind there was was against them, they weren't making much progress. The beach seemed very empty and lonely without Christina, but I soon relaxed and began to enjoy myself. Went for a walk singing '*Les feuilles mortes*' as I went along: '*et la mer efface sur le sable les pas des amants désunis*', looking back to watch the sea sweep away my footprints. I suddenly felt something was amiss and turned round to see in a tree, amongst the branches, a bag, like mine, hanging there. The sight was a shock, like Robinson discovering Friday's footprints. I realised that someone must be in the bushes, and that person wanted me to know they were there. I rushed back to my mat, pulled on my shorts and then realised that my bag was missing. A mixture of anger and fear arose in my throat. I looked at the bag in the tree and recognised it to be my own. I carefully walked up to it, looking out for man traps and shouting that I wasn't happy and that I was going to kill someone. Hopefully that would frighten them away or I'd have to stand and fight. From the footprints there was only one person anyway so I hedged my bets and hoped he wouldn't be that big. I grabbed my bag, folded my things and trotted away looking behind me. When I'd got further away I started to check my bag. Nothing was amiss, my money was in my pockets, my cheap disposable camera and my clothes were still there. It was a strange practical joke or a warning. Ever since Cuba was discovered the natives must have been playing similar jokes on the new arrivals. A light hearted warning reminding us who is boss and whose land this is.

When I got back to the main beach I told the security guard, who remembered me, or rather he remembered I had been there with

Christina, what had happened. He only laughed and said, 'I told you so,' then asked me for a tip. Why he should think I would give him a tip for pointing out how stupid I am I don't know.

I went to the tourists' bit and sat gloomily with my clothes on behind four European girls, who turned out to be Danish. They were kind enough to talk to me before I spoke to them and I asked them to watch my stuff while I went for a swim, telling them about what just happened. I went in the sea and soon one of the girls followed me. Just as she was telling me about her plans to travel the world I felt a sharp sting on my bum. It made me jump and I asked a local what it could be. He told me not to worry but the jellyfish always get stirred up after much rain. I went and sat down, or rather lay down on my belly until Yvette turned up. By now the stinging had died down. She offered to urinate on the flesh wound for me to cure the sting. I told her that I preferred the pain but thanked her anyway. I think Yvette might be a bit kinky!

I've just seen El Muchacho. He snubbed me on the beach earlier on (he was with his young friends). He came to see what I was doing. There is a definite sense of friendship developing there, if he wasn't half my age I'm sure we'd be great friends. He's just the sort I would have hung around with when I was 18. Though I was more handsome than he is! I've asked Dave to bring him some porn. Pornography is illegal in Cuba, that's probably why there are so many street wankers. Then again everything seems to be illegal in Cuba, except loud music, the neighbours are playing Ragaton so loud my bed is shaking!

Just spent 15 minutes dancing ragaton in front of the mirror in my boxers. I think I look quite sexy! Though my thighs are killing now.

God I keep getting distracted from the important things, all these pretty boys and girls and sexy music! I forgot to mention the police checking every Cuban's ID papers last night. I asked around and eventually got the discreet answer, '*Hay un barco*'. I don't know if the boat was for last night or if it had already left but obviously it was important enough for the police to check if all the youngsters were still in Trinidad. I don't know why they were only checking the young Cubans who were enjoying themselves or if there had been a tip off!

I just walked four beautiful, drunken Danish girls to the door of La Cuava. I left them there. I think it was the best thing to do. It is strange to see so many groups of women. Very few all male groups of tourists.

Day 35

I tried to buy the Elegguá necklace: $2 seems a lot to me for a piece of plastic. I went to the library today. There was a whole army of librarians (about ten) behind the desk and about five borrowers (is that what you call someone who goes to the library?). When I got my book and sat down to read *La Historia de Cuba* (2001), it is interesting to get the official history of a country, a young librarian came over and made me sign and date a register. When I left I took the book back to the shelf and noticed the same librarian huff, shrug her shoulders and go to find the book. I think that was the only thing she did all day.

I've just got a burning stomach and wind, still fasting everyday between breakfast and dinner, hopefully this will help, though I really want food today more often than usual, apparently there is a stomach bug going around Trinidad at the moment.

'*Donde los hombres tienen corazón, tuviera el estrella.*'

Just told P de la Casa Particular that I hope he didn't mind Yvette coming round. He said of course not and if I want to be left alone with her I only need to close the door. Though she can't stop the night!

Elegguá likes to play tricks and torment vain men. Perhaps it was Elegguá who took my bag while I was wandering naked along the beach. Vanity.

I hope the *Santanero* that I'm going to meet tomorrow is a real one.

I've just eaten loads yet still feel hungry. I wonder if I may have a bug.

Day 36

Spanish lesson cool, spent most of the lesson chatting to the 5-year-old boy who wouldn't believe me that his Snoopy dog was called Snoopy. Then listened to some Columbian Country and Western. On the way home a cute mulatta came up to me and asked if I remembered her. This took me back a little and she told me we'd met in Camagüäy. She seemed very surprised when I told her I wasn't Cuban. I seem to be blending in. Another year in Cuba and I'll be leading the Cubans in a new wave, new age counter revolution, anti imperialist and anti communist, sounds like Anarchy, and I might even get laid.

I went to see the market girl who was going to introduce me to her uncle who is a *Santanero*. He wasn't there, she told me he was in the country doing the magic, with animals etc. I told her not to worry I'd go and buy a plastic necklace. She wasn't happy and assured me her uncle would be there tomorrow. Smells like a lie to me, I don't think I'll bother going tomorrow. Apparently there is a place of Orisha worship that tourists keep telling me about, I'll see if I can find it. Though it isn't that important, just gives me something to do.

Yvette didn't turn up when she said she would, for the second time. Am I the only person who keeps his word? Anyway I'm learning not to.

I spoke to Dave this morning, it was good to hear a familiar voice. He's got his visa and is looking forward to coming over, so am I. It will be good to spend time with someone who isn't after my money. Still I would like to meet some more Cubans, J doesn't seem to want to introduce me to her friends, or they're not that interested in me.

I just went to the Orisha shop. I got talking to the man in his front room who sells paraphernalia for the Orishas. He explained to me what the various objects were for. There were lead moulded guns; knives and keys (a bit like the pieces in a Cluedo set) there were various bits of wood, leaves (laurel I think) and candle mobiles, the ones that move around when heat rises underneath them. He told me that I can make a shrine to Balé Oyé (St Lazarus). It was a pile of dried mud with stones for eyes, nose and mouth, underneath was a tray where he could put offerings. It seems like quite a gentle form of Voodoo.

When I came out of the shop I saw the same market girl, who had tried to fix me up with her uncle, walking towards the shop. Coincidence! The shop is the other side of town to the market. I quickly turned away and walked down the street.

When I got back, I proudly showed my wares to the lady of the house. She looked at me almost in disgust and asked what I wanted with those. She is a practising Catholic and found it hard to see the funny side. People really take the Afro-Cuban religion seriously and she made it clear that Orisha worship was a thing for negroes. I bought a necklace (that I cut down to make a bracelet as well), pieces of hard wood, some sort of palisander, that I'm going to carve it into an Elegguá, and some relaxing balsam, that is made from oil but has no distinctive smell.

I feel a bit self-conscious about wearing the necklace, I'm not used to wearing jewellery and I wonder whether it isn't a bit like wearing a rosary.

Here's some good Cuban music as recommended by El Muchacho:

Gente de Zona	EDK, Clan 537 – Ragaton (Habana)
Charangu Habuuera	Los Ban Ban, Mumolito Simonel y Su Trabujo
Bomboleo	Pupi y los que son son – Salsa

I finished my little figurine of Elegguá. It looks like a very crude African statue. Hard wood and difficult to carve with a jack knife.

I read an article by Ambrosio Formet, a Cuban scholar. The article states how fed up Cuban artists and writers are at being given so little space to express themselves. Ever since the Revolution culture has been considered one of the least important facets of Cuban society after the economy, health, education, agriculture, infra-structure etc. Literature is almost considered anti-cultural by the Communist bureaucracy because it gives more importance to aesthetics than politics, and there is a confrontation between the two. Most Cuban writers live abroad and therefore mean little to the young Cubans today.

It must be very difficult to write in a country where there is so little freedom of speech. I'm sure Ché, who was quite cultivated, would have been disappointed by the lack of theatres, cinemas, modern art and modern writing. Cuban society is stifled by bureaucracy at every turn. Ironically this is leading to a rise in imperialistic attitudes among young Cubans, whose only idea of cultural experience is to watch an American movie, which are shown nearly every night on TV!

Day 37

8 am power cut

Spanish lessons. Day on the beach, good swim, saw the same Cuban girl who thought I was Cuban yesterday. She wouldn't leave me alone until I took her phone number, she's not very bright, doesn't seem clever enough to be interested financially and seems to genuinely fancy me. Can't be much over 20, I wonder if I'm being seduced Cuban style. She certainly won't take no for an answer, I should have told her I have a girlfriend here, but it was so nice to talk to someone new, someone who was treating me like a Cuban. Though I think she might be a pain. I'll ask J what to do. I think she is mad.

I'm taking my mid-life crisis like a man, going to the beach every other day, swimming a kilometre and working on a really great tan. I'll carry on flirting with every young woman I can until something happens. When Dave comes we'll take a couple of girls out for the night. I know Dave is turning into a lonely old divorcee, so fuck it we'll just have fun. I might not have found anything to die for here in Cuba but I've found a lot to live for!

I was pestered for about half hour on *la escalinatar* by one of those scruffy, scabbied, flea-bitten dogs that are everywhere in Cuba. I learnt a while ago not to touch them, I'm covered in fleas again, and when I got back to my door there was another one that wouldn't stop jumping on me until I pushed it away with my foot. I've never kicked a dog before and I found it difficult to do but it was the only thing I could do, it was so insistent. I think I'm going to have to do something with the Chica Loca, I'm not here to entertain her and she's not my problem, neither are all the half-starved dogs in the country.

I had been hoping to meet some of J's Cuban friends but she just turned up with a load more tourists.

Day 38

Saint John's Day

My fourth wisdom tooth is nearly through and is giving me teething pains, it's sore and bleeding. If the dentist had not insisted on capping the tooth in front I bet my wisdom tooth would be through by now!

30 mins on Internet with no connection. I changed 30 dollars for 24 CUC, that's a bad rate of exchange and means I have less money than I thought. I can't remember who gave me the tip of bringing US$ to Cuba but it must have been a long time since they were here.

Went for a long walk north, north east of the town. As I was walking along one of the overhead power cables, that had recently been replaced (this is the reason for all the power cuts), suddenly exploded and fell to the ground writhing around like a wounded snake spitting sparks and flames until it went dead. This is probably another reason for all the power cuts!

I saw the usual horse-drawn taxis and cowboys, many bareback riding. It was hot, probably the hottest since I've been here in Trinidad, which is appropriate for mid-summer.

I've been having difficulties trying to explain that today is the longest day. It is probably only longer than the shortest day by about 40 minutes so this doesn't make much difference to Cubans.

I was going to go for a walk in the mountains this weekend but Carnival sounds quite fun. So far I've had it described to me in various ways. There is a procession with dancers on floats, music and puppets all different colours. The taxi driver yesterday told me that all the cowboys ride in from the country, drink lots of rum, get into fights and fall over in the gutter. P of the *Casa Particular* reckons he's going to stay in all weekend because there will be so many drunks fighting, stabbing and robbing each other. So far all I've seen is the usual street market, open late with lots of homemade beer being passed around.

I saw a funny sign in the service station on the way back, there was a warning sign with a bottle with a line going through it underneath the sign was written 'No drinking rum'.

I met El Muchacho today. He told me he is going blind. Not a lie! It doesn't take much to scratch away at the surface and discover the human being below, with all their trials and tribulations. Poor kid, he's handsome and charming, the best dancer I've ever seen. Always surrounded by beautiful young women that he can hardly see. This also explains why he's snubbed me twice on the beach. I thought he'd prefer to be drinking with his mates and pretty girls than talking to someone twice his age. He came up to me today to make sure I'd be going to La Cuava with him and his friends tomorrow night. That is just kindness. Now I've got to know Cubans they are quite simply among the kindest people I've ever met. There is no way I would have made an effort to hang around with a foreigner twice my age when I was 18.

I'm going to try to give him English lessons, if he speaks English he may be able to get into a tourist school and not spend his life behind a bar serving drunken Cubans. Not much time though.

As far as his sight is concerned he is in the best country for curing weak eyes. I've met quite a few foreigners, Canadians, Latin Americans, Swiss and Germans who are here for eye treatment.

Silvio Rodriguez: Unicornio azul:
My blue unicorn has gone away
He's gone onto pastures new, and disappeared
Without leaving any news:
Even though I paid, the flowers he left behind,
He didn't want to talk to me.
My blue unicorn has gone away
I don't know if he's left me or if he's lost.
And I no longer have a blue unicorn
I pray anyone to give me news I'll pay
100,000 and 1 million
My blue unicorn was lost to me yesterday, it left.
My blue unicorn and I had a friendship
A little with love, a little with truth . . .

Well that was the most peaceful Midsummer's Day I've spent in years.

Day 39

Lessons in the morning. Gave J a French lesson then I went to buy a shirt. The shop was full of assistants (three) but the door was closed. When I shouted through the window that I wanted to come in they said it was closed. I think they just close when they want to, it doesn't make any difference to them if they sell anything or not, they still get paid the same. I told the girl through the window, that I needed a shirt, she sent me to the shop opposite, even though her shop is the only one in Trinidad to sell shirts, not T-shirts.

There is not much sign of a Carnival except that the music is three times louder than usual. I still don't have a shirt to wear tonight. The two I brought with me are ripped or stained.

No shirt worth buying (20 CUC).

I met the Quebecois couple I'd met on the beach earlier, and we went around the fairground attractions. Big wheel, roller coaster, all worn and rusted, left over from the Russian times, obviously made in Soviet Russia from big heavy duty machinery. The machinery reminded me of a Russian camera I bought in the 80s, it was too heavy to take decent pictures without a tripod but when I dropped it down the side of a mountain it survived quite intact, with only a few scratches. Anyway these rides, although small and slow, looked more dangerous than any I'd seen before. Most of them were supported by makeshift scaffolding and wobbled frighteningly as they moved. Ate a pizza and drank orange juice, which may prove to be a mistake (I've been burping non stop now for an hour).

10 pm and 34°C

First time in Cuba when there has been no wind. It's suffocating. I had dinner and drank half a bottle of rum with my friend whose birthday it is. I left him to sleep it off. I'm still burping a lot even after so much food. It's difficult to find any energy in this heat. I want to go clubbing but my legs are too heavy and my stomach is too bloated.

There is one thing worse than having diarrhoea and that is thinking all night that you do because of the burning stomach, not dancing, smiling sweetly instead of talking and then finding out once you get home that you don't have diarrhoea! I do have a burning stomach.

One thing I'd like to remember is El Muchacho dancing salsa with his brother, they've obviously danced together for years because they were better dancing with each other than with any girl. They did it so naturally, only Cuban men can dance salsa together without looking gay. Except the gay Cubans who look really gay even more like women than any woman I've seen.

I'm going to stop writing this diary now because I realise that it is becoming a barrier between me and these people I like so much. I'm thinking more about what I'm going to put into the diary, rather than enjoying the moment. I'm even calling people by the names I've given them in this book. I'm constantly wondering if I can do things in case reporting what I do or what other people do will compromise myself or them. The whole of my stay here in Cuba is a compromise, to some extent. Dropping out of the routine I got into in Europe, although intended as an extended holiday it has now become a life-changing experience. This pause comes at a time when I needed to sit back and take stock of what I have done so far in my life, remember the people I have loved, the places I have lived in, the work I have done. What does it all mean? Quite simply my stay here in Cuba has showed me that it doesn't mean anything, I'm happier now sitting here on the patio waiting for the humming birds to come sniffing around the scarlet jasmine, or the butterflies to flutter by inconstantly, ceaselessly bringing my soul to life, inspiring me to put pen to paper. Maybe even to share these words with friends or family. What I can do now is open my heart, because I've never been so in touch with my heart before. The words block and expression fails but right here and now I've found a self-love that will endure many years after my return from Cuba. El Muchaco and la Chica, la Playa de Ancon, will one day be a distant memory but I will always have changed and grown out of this experience. Cuba too is going to change, Castro won't be long before he retires and though the government who support him will take over, the young people of Cuba will eventually overthrow his out-dated politics. I hope for the Cuban people that the change will be for the better. I wish them all good and only want to express my views of life here to give them support. What worries me the most is that all will change for the worse, the threat of America will grow, the new government will want to tighten-up on the people, the oppressive observation and control of the people, in what after all is a communist regime, will lead to arrests, financial penalties, job prospects made less hopeful or any other of the unwritten threats by the Cuban officials will be carried through, and somehow simple words of respect will be misinterpreted or used against the very people they are trying to support.

This isn't a eulogy to the Cuban people but I'm poignantly aware that talking openly about anything that happens in Cuba today could be used by the government, that is why most people don't want to talk. These people have taken me into their confidence and I don't want to exploit that for my own benefit. I should just stop writing, and get on with this extended holiday, take full advantage of the little time I have here before my money and my visa run out.

The main reason I'm keeping this journal is to have a constant reminder of what I'm experiencing. And yes, also to share this experience with others. All my friends will want to know what life is really like out here, and I'll just send them a copy of this journal.

This break in life has been time for pause, to step out of the routine, school, work, retirement. Forget about it all and find myself. Get away from the institution that is Europe, that easy way of life where you just sit back and do as you're told and everything is looked after for you. From the tearful moment you step in through those overwhelmingly large wooden doors at primary school to be herded along from one class to another, from one year to another, to university and work, yet another institution that pays your way as long as it's the way they want. Always being rewarded for being the best to conform, certificates to say how good you are at learning what they tell you is the truth, and money, house, car and all the other clutter that just gets in the way of life until you've got bags of it all, tons of stuff that show how good you are at living someone else's life; the life that was prescribed to you before you were even born.

Yet here, a million miles away from all that, I can forget it, I'm just left here with me and my heart, open to myself for the first time ever and more open to the world than it has ever been before. Reborn.

Reminds me of the old Buddhist tale of the monk who visits a strange land. When he arrives at the border he asks for a guide to show him around during his travels. They see many interesting and new sights but what preoccupies the monk the most is the cemetery. For as far as one can see there are individual burial mounds and at the head of each mound is a pile of large smooth stones. Some mounds have as few as two rocks deliberately placed there and some have as many as ten or fifteen, very few have more than that. The monk turns to the guide and asks why there are stones there. The guide explains that the stones represent the amount of time the person lived before they died. The monk is astounded and sadly observes that there are so many young people and children buried in this vast burial site.

'Oh no,' the guide corrects him, 'these are not children, we place a stone there for every year the person has really lived during their life.'

And so I want to live, I have never been afraid of dying but now even more I want to live my life as I choose fit for me, without all the trappings of my education, religion, or social upbringing. I want to do it my way, as the old song goes. And I'd better hurry up. Most of my life has been spent worrying about others, helping others in times of need, though completely ignoring my own needs. Looking good in the eyes of others, then trying to look good. But now I don't really give a damn, it's as though time is running out and I want to stop living for others and live for myself, my joy, fill my own heart with love, experience the here and now for me and not worry about what is going to happen to others tomorrow. That's just a life of never being here now but always waiting for tomorrow, and as Janis Joplin wisely points out 'tomorrow never comes'. Love myself now, fill my heart with joy now, let my soul come to the surface and breathe for herself. Fill myself with life and love, and when my heart overflows then I can give the excess to others, those around me, then, when my heart is full I can give freely without expecting anything in return, without needing anything in return, just let go, let go of all the stuff and live my life, freely, joyfully. That is the way forward.

This is very difficult because I want to cherish every moment here, but writing about life isn't living it so I'm going to stop writing now!

EL HABANERO

The following story I began writing on the plane back from Cuba. It is based on my experiences when I went to stay with A's family in the countryside. Most of what I describe I saw for myself, the rest is hearsay. The family live in a little pueblo in the interior of the island and on the edge of one of the many sugar plantations. Again I was taken into the hearts of these people who opened their homes to me as though it was my own. The journey to get there itself was an adventure, some of which I describe below. The journey back was quite simply painful and filled with nausea and illness.

The people there had nothing by wealthy Western standards, yet they had so much that people in wealthy countries are crying out for. The love and fondness that I experienced in this *pueblito*, between the villagers, was moving, all looked out for the children, sometimes it was difficult to tell whose children belonged to whom; everyone would take them in and it was up to everyone to put them in their place. Living so close to nature the harmony with the forest was not contrived but necessary. Quite simply, out here the government does not provide enough, and to live to a reasonable standard people have to live from the land. Trade and barter is practised openly and is the only form of exchange. I was invited crocodile hunting, but only if one escaped from the swamp into the river, and as exciting as this sounds it really only meant a gang of drunken young men wandering through the remains of a tropical jungle armed with harpoons, lassoes and a bottle of rum each. I don't think they really knew how to catch a crocodile. Though, again, I heard rumours; rumours of boots and handbags that had been made from the carcass of these animals caught by brave villagers in the past. I only saw one crocodile skin suitcase, that could have come from anywhere in the world. The dog fight I did witness and this is quite common in Cuba, I also witnessed the slaughtering of a goat, in my honour, even though I'd explained during the whole week that I was vegetarian. I was taken to collect wild honey that came from stingless bees. Most of the things I describe in this short story seemed stranger than fiction at the time.

After all, this whole diary was inspired by Hemingway, he described what he witnessed in Cojimar; the old man so like many of the local sailors I've seen on the coast. This 'Old Man' was probably a little older than me when Hemingway wrote the book, and quite surprisingly went on to live to be over a hundred, according to local legend. So much of my short life here appears as fiction, so much of what I write is based on hearsay and rumour that it is difficult to separate fiction from fact. The difficulty lies not only in the oppressive structure of the omnipresent, communist big brother infringing on our freedom of speech, but more in the act of writing itself. I'm sure everything Hemingway wrote in his book was true, the sharks ate the swordfish, I've seen sharks hunting swordfish since I've been here. I may have seen the very boat the Old Man sailed out in to catch the legendary bait. I certainly went to Cuba to find it. And what I found was a country full of legend; from Colombus landing, in what he thought to be India, to the present-day subterfuge of the illegal American settlement in Guantanamo and the questionable incarceration of suspected terrorists, Cuba has always appeared as a country full of mystery juxtaposed with history where, quite frankly, it is difficult to separate truth from fiction and very easy to marry the two. How can I go on writing the truth when the truth is so difficult to discern and the possible repercussion of speaking openly so worrying?

The following account I've written in story form to avoid compromising my friends and their family. I still don't know today whether my stay with them was legal. I do know that it was of the greatest kindness.

1: THE END OF THE JOURNEY

'*Amigo, aqui e la casa de Piedro.*' The horse driver spoke nonchalantly as though stating the more than obvious, even though the house had been empty for more than thirty years.

'*Gracias.*' His legs nearly gave way as he jumped from the hot metal cart. The cart trundled away along the dark ochre dirt 'rack that ran along the edge of the forest. The dirt track stretched away into the distance on one side the forest, on the other a sugar plantation that faded gently into the obscure horizon. The sun was peering out suspiciously from behind the palms that were entangled in vines and other trees. The straw roofs of wooden shacks could be seen interspersed in among the trees or next to the sugar canes that reached almost as high as the houses themselves. All was calm. The constant breeze seemed to have died

82

down. There wasn't a cloud in the sky. The peace and quiet seemed tangible and enveloped him in calm warmth. He stood there and looked at the building in front of him; a wooden shack with two windows at the front as high and as wide as the door they stood by. It was crowned with a straw roof like the others nearby but this roof was worn and battered by time. He slowly wiped the sweat from his face and stepped under the thatched porch to get out of the sun.

The sun had been blazing down on him for three days now, his only relief from the heat being the shade of the slave trees that grew on the edge of each village he had walked through, the only beautiful remains of a sad history. How many men had lived and died under the shelter of the huge dark green trees with their dense foliage that spread out flat at the base, the only shelter from the heat and from the rain. Now hundreds of years old they stood solitary and majestic, no longer nourished by the sweat and blood of men. The trees were happy for the company of this lonely traveller as he slept, exhausted, beneath their protective boughs.

Three days by road; bus, car, lorry and the rest by foot, he'd been travelling now for nearly a week looking for the village Miguel's granddad had told him about. Now, as he stood on the dusty threshold of a new life, he hesitated before turning the handle. A parrot was squawking in the thick green forest beyond what was once a back yard, now overgrown with Jasmine and Bougainvillea; domesticity run wild. It wasn't his house but where else could he go, his family couldn't help him, his friends in Havana might get arrested if they were caught with him, he just needed to lie low before he tried to get out of the country. His hand lifted itself mechanically and pushed the door open. Everything must be in the same place as thirty years ago, when Miguel's granddad Piedro had left for Habana to join his wife's family. He squeezed through the doorway because the rusty hinges prevented the door from opening further. Inside strips of bright, white light poured in through the gaps between the planks that were crudely nailed together to make the walls.

Two wooden rocking chairs waited patiently beside a wooden box that must have been the dining table, an enamelled tin mug still sat there ready for the next coffee to be served. Apart from the old bed on the concrete floor, in the cornered off part of the shack that served as a bedroom, this was the only furniture in the house. Amaurie went through to the empty kitchen and pushed open the back door. The garden had grown right up over the back porch and it took a few minutes before he could get through. Beyond the overgrowth he could make out the silhouette of a chain and pulley on the metal arch of the well. He couldn't get to it this way because of the undergrowth, so decided to walk back round via the front of the shack. The path from the road to the well was a little more worn and he reached it just as the sun was going down. He dropped the bucket 20 foot or so into the water, rinsed it out, filled it again, sniffed the water, tasted a little, it seemed safe enough, and plunged his head in, cool and refreshing. He then emptied the bucket, took out the small packet from inside his shirt that was wrapped in plastic bags tied on with flaxen string, and dropped it into the bucket. This he then slowly lowered about ten feet and jammed the chain between two heavy rocks, and returned inside.

He slept heavily, feeling protected by his wooden shelter, in spite of the solid concrete floor that dug into his hips and shoulders. The bed was still damp from a leaking roof and there seemed to be something living in the mattress. Cockroaches. Twice during the night he'd been disturbed by a large toad that slid its way in under the lower planks that served as a wall and croaked loudly in his ear. This toad was to become a common bed companion for most of his stay.

Something echoed in his mind, something of importance. And although he heard the clank, clank, clank of the chains as they passed through the pulley he paid as little attention as if it had been someone else's alarm clock. Eventually he got up. Still drowsy, thirsty, hungry, he opened the front door, stepped onto the porch, reached in his pocket for his final cigarette, lit it and blew the smoke at the half risen sun. Standing in front of the sun was the dark solid megalithic shape of an old man in an old straw hat and worn out old clothes. The man remained still, staring at the front door as though no one had come through it. His skin was nearly black and deeply wrinkled by a life of working in the sugarcane fields. '*Que hola?*' shouted Amaurie, blowing smoke at the large worn leather boots. 'Is this yours?' said the croaky old voice, that reminded Amaurie a little of the toad the night before. A worn, ingrained hand the size of a shovel held out the packet that Amaurie had gone to so little trouble to hide.

'*Si es el mio,*' and he stepped forward and took it quickly, suspiciously eyeing the old man who just stood staring back with kind eyes that had obviously seen too much of life to be worried about the triflings of this young man.

'So you're Pepe's grandson?'

'*Si,*' hesitated Amaurie, biting his lip and hoping this would be the last lie he ever had to tell. Something in the kind old brown eyes looking back at him inspired a sense of honesty. All his life he'd been telling lies and he hoped that here, at last, he could start over again a new honest life. At school they taught him to say things he didn't believe in and the better he told lies the more prizes he got. The glorious revolution, Ché and Fidel our glorious leaders and martyrs in the war against Imperialism. Lies, lies he felt, though he didn't know any other truth. Then, as he grew up and the tourists began to arrive in Havana, he knew this was the only way to gain anything. He and Miguel were quick to learn English and soon started charming the tourists.

A professional Jintanero knows his town first. He knows every area worth seeing and many more not worth seeing. He knows every back alley or derelict building for a quick escape, and every late night bar or bordello in Havana.

But most of all he knows the tourists. Just looking at the tourists he could tell how much they were worth and where to take them to get the most out of them. The quickest score is the Japanese. They may seem the hardest because they never speak English or any other European language, but this is also an advantage. A quick robbery in downtown Buena Vista, then they spend two days in the police station trying to explain what happened, eventually getting fed up with Cuban bureaucracy and wanting to get on with their holiday. The Germans took longest, you really had to work hard to scam a German, they are very tight with their money and it takes them a long time to get drunk, but girls usually loosen them up and their wallets too, and once they get spending they really do spend and give good tips too. Italians are easy, just give them a black whore and charge double. English and Canadians are the easiest pickings and fall for any scam that involves them thinking they're making a profit; false notes, antiques, false cigars, anything they think they can sell for more back home, and they probably do. The French always fall for food and drink, take them to a friend's bar and charge them twice the price all night. Other Europeans usually fit into one of these categories, and any scam can be helped by taking them out dancing with pretty Cuban boys or pretty Cuban girls.

All this seemed irrelevant now in front of these kind old eyes that had probably known nothing but the peace and tranquillity of village life.

'*Si pero* . . . Piedro is dead.'

'Yes I know . . . Last I saw him he'd gone to La Habana.'

'Yes.'

'Well when you're ready I'll help you get settled, that's my house behind yours, we share the same well,' and he slowly turned and walked off towards another shack with a palm straw roof in the distance. For some reason he stopped to kick a derelict bus that lay along the side of the dirt path.

In the house Amaurie was already counting the money. 160 American dollars, 480 euros, 320 pounds which works out as 1260 CUC – 30,264 in national money, all there, the old man hadn't even opened the packet.

2: THE HOME

Amaurie spent the rest of the day tidying the place up. One by one the villagers turned up to see Piedro's grandson, each time bringing something useful or offering to help him settle in. A metal bucket, a stick-bristled broom, a clean rag, he was given help connecting to the electricity and someone even gave him a broken television set. A new, or rather less mouldy and infested, mattress was given to him. They brought him food too; mangoes, bananas, bomba fruit, papas, malangas, yucca and rice. He placed the rusty old cast iron pan on the fire he had lit on the porch and ate warm food for the first time in days. It was delicious. The rice seemed to melt in his mouth and the boiled pork tasted almost sweet. He even had coffee, and this was just what he needed to bring himself around. He was beginning to feel himself again and was more convivial with his new neighbours who didn't stop all day coming to introduce themselves and welcome him.

The villagers were kind but each of them came out with the same refrain: 'I'm Catholic and in the eyes of God we are all brothers, so I give you this present, my brother, so that you may stay among us and share in village life.' And each invited him to their home to come and talk. There were 60 homes in the village and Amaurie was glad of the company. He decided to spend the week getting to know his new neighbours. Carlos lived nearest, or at least it was his barn that backed onto the overgrown garden. He was younger than Amaurie, about 30, with three children and a serious looking wife. When it came to using the toilet Amaurie was sent into the back garden where the whole family went to pee. There was a latrine, a 15 ft hole in the ground to shit into, but they rarely used it. The garden was used for everything; toilet, compost, the animals were butchered there, the blood soaking into the ground. Flies everywhere! And this is where the children played and everyone walked barefoot. Amaurie was surprised at the lack of awareness of hygiene. The children always seemed to be ill, with runny noses or stomach upsets. This didn't surprise him and he felt angry. Only the day before, Carlos, his wife and the two children had travelled 60 kilometres in the back of a tractor to get to the nearest doctor. The doctor confirmed that the children had a fever and sent them away again with medicine not explaining what the medicine did. In spite of their illness the parents continued to feed the children fresh milk. 'What they need is oranges,' Amaurie told the family. 'Oranges and honey, vitamin C will help the children fight the flu.'

'*Naranjas* . . . we've lots of *naranjas*,' said Carlos, somewhat surprised at the prescription. 'The doctor didn't mention oranges or any food for that matter. We'll go and get *naranjas* right now – you can help us collect them, the nearest tree with ripe oranges is in the forest.' The two men strolled into the forest in silence both contemplating the issue in hand, as though they had a mission to do and the lives of these children depended on them gathering as many oranges as possible. Of course this wasn't the case but they still managed to fill two sacks with fresh oranges. They dropped the oranges off at the house, picked up a syringe and, accompanied by another villager (Carlos' cousin), they headed back into the forest, though down a different, less worn path. Stepping over the undergrowth and pushing aside the huge leaves of the banana trees to get through, eventually they came to a large trunk that had fallen down but was resting on a smaller tree so as not to touch the ground.'Don't worry, the bees don't sting.'

Amaurie wasn't convinced and stood back a distance as the two men pulled away at the bark to reveal the hive inside the dead trunk. Bees flew everywhere and soon Carlos' hands were covered, he very gently brushed them off with the same care that one would brush away a butterfly. Inside the trunk were little waxen pods. The syringe was stuck into the pods to suck out the runny honey. After some time of going through the same process they had filled an empty rum bottle with clear yellow honey.

'*Te gusta?*' Carlos' cousin asked, offering the syringe half full, and Amaurie squeezed the amber nectar onto his tongue. It was the sweetest honey he had ever tasted.

Back at Carlos' shack his wife told Amaurie how the following day she and some friends would take some honey and cover each other in it to give themselves smooth skin. This was the best way for women to treat their skin and they did it as often as possible, but usually they couldn't afford to do so as the honey was food for the children. But this time there was enough honey to go round and the bees would be hard at it producing more in the near future.

'So what do we do with the oranges?' Carlos questioned, genuinely interested, as though he was asking a pharmacist how to take the medicine.

Amaurie was shocked, how far removed these people had come from their heritage. From the thickness of their hair, their physiognomy and the flecks in their pupils most people in the village were descendants from Spanish and Arawaks. But the Arawak had been taken away from them, subdued and oppressed until they even believed themselves that they were no more descendants from the indigenous peoples. For generations everything had been done for them, in school they are taught how to behave like good citizens, but what do these people know about city life, descendants of Spanish farm workers and native Americans. The Revolution meant nothing to them, it had just taken away their peasant knowledge and left them with meaningless jargon about anti-imperialism.

'Squeeze the oranges and mix in some honey and give this to the kids before they eat. And stop feeding them milk, that is only feeding the cold.'

The parents listened, concerned for their children and respectful of this city wisdom. Which it wasn't really, it was just what Amaurie had been told by his Grandma.

'God bless you,' said Carlos' wife, and fell to her knees in front of a faded picture of the virgin *de la Caridad*, in pure religious fervour, rocking backwards and forwards on her knees, reciting what sounded like the Our Father, though muttered so low it was difficult to tell.

Whatever the intellectual education hadn't taken away from them, Catholicism did. No longer did they worship the sun, the moon and the sea but obeyed the Catholic Church to the letter, fearing continuously to fall into some superstitious practice or other.

Amaurie had come across Catholicism and many other religions, in a country where all religions are tolerated and practised openly this was quite common, but such religious fervour was unusual in the city.

'We need to leave,' Carlos began, 'we need to go to the city. There is no future here for the children just the same as in the past, the children need educating but their teacher never comes to the town school, she has to walk ten kilometres and the state won't even provide a bicycle. And now it's a day's journey to see the doctor and the doctor isn't always there. Life here is simple but the children need more.'

Amaurie nodded in sympathy, but couldn't help asking the question that was growing in his mind:

'When did the police last come to the village?'

'I've never seen a policeman here, they sometimes go to the town and once a man was arrested at the sugar factory for killing his wife, but otherwise the police don't come here.'

'Well my friend,' he changed the subject, pointing to the two-year-old and the six-year-old boys, 'they seem to like your drink – look they've finished it all up. I'll get them some more, and tonight we'll drink some sugar cane rum made by El Zonzon, the strongest alcohol in the whole of Cuba.'

No sooner had the bottle been placed on the patio floor and the first two glasses been served than El Zonzon himself turned up. El Zonzon looked even older than El Viejo, the old neighbour who had greeted him this morning, but apparently he was younger, the alcohol and tobacco had had an effect.

'*Buena dia* – you must be Piedro's grandson . . . What's your name?'

'Miguel,' lied Amaurie, pinching his inner thigh as he spoke. He hated lying to these people who spoke so openly and had nothing and therefore had nothing to hide.

'Good name,' came the reply and the Zonzon just sat there and stared at Amaurie gently nodding his head as though he had been talking to an old friend and suddenly ran out of things to say. He picked up the bottle and filled his glass.

'Do you have any tobacco Miguel, Piedro's grandson?'

'No I don't, sorry, I smoked my last cigarette.'

'Don't worry.' He leant back on his low stool, stretching his right hand far back behind his head and from the dark another hand reached forward and gently offered a cigarette. How long El Viejo had been standing there Amaurie didn't know, his dark skin and clothes were difficult to see in the penumbra of the fluorescent light that was dangled precariously from a beam above them. He greeted Amaurie with a smile before sitting down. Apart from this friendly gesture El Viejo ignored El Zonzon completely. Then Carlos' uncle and cousin turned up and the rum went very quickly. El Zonzon began his usual diatribe about the Revolution which the others listened to patiently, the same speech they must have heard a thousand times. The Revolution made no difference to the country folk, before they worked for a Spanish landlord and earned very little money, now they earned 20 Cuban *pesos* a day working for the government, his father had been right telling him not to get involved in the war against Baptista and the Americans, nothing would come of it and nothing did, not for us, here in the country.

'And who is going to listen to us? Who is going to tell the government in La Habana what life is like here for us in the country? We don't get to meet foreigners and receive foreign money. We're lucky if our rations arrive on time. No, nothing has changed for us my friend.'

Once the bottle was empty, El Zonzon stood up and walked off into the darkness, wandering home, blindly following the same well trodden path like an owl flying in the pitch black.

The jungle echoed in the background, frogs and toads croaked, somewhere a dove cooed, late to bed.

Amaurie now noticed that El Viejo was wearing not one but three shirts while the younger men sat there topless. He found it hard to move in the damp heat without breaking out into a sweat.

'Do you like catfish?' asked Carlos as if to make a point.

'Yes I think so but I haven't eaten it for a long time,' lied Amaurie from habit.

'What about crocodile, do you eat crocodile?' Said Carlos' uncle.

'That I never have,' laughed Amaurie, who thought they were joking.

'Well we will start with catfish, tomorrow you will come fishing with us.'

And all three men stood up and went to bed leaving the young stranger wondering what to do. He fumbled his way back to his shack in the pitch dark and slid into bed listening to the croak, croak, croak of the toad next to him that sang him to sleep.

3: THE VILLAGE

The sound of someone walking around in the front room woke Amaurie up. It was unlike the villagers to enter someone's house unannounced. After six weeks he was getting used to their customs, though not the well water.

'*Que hola quien es?*'

No-one answered, just a shuffle to the back room which served as a kitchen. He reached for the machete, which he kept jammed between two boards on the wall, and slowly climbed out of the window to walk around to the back room. If there was someone there he wanted to catch them. Maybe El Viejo had talked, let it slip about the money, perhaps the whole village knew by now and someone was just waiting for the right time to make their move. He quickly pulled open the door and jumped into the kitchen wielding his machete clumsily. Something moved and ran at him, he dodged to the left and swung the large blade at the dark, low figure that seemed to duck. The flat of the blade smacked against solid flesh and with a loud, high-pitched trumpeting sound, the pig, about 300 lbs, charged Amaurie, flipping him over its back and careering out of the back door into the garden beyond. This surprised the young man and the comedy of the situation left him in hysterics as he rolled around, giggling like a young child being tickled, on the hard black floor.

Within an hour Carlos' wife brought him breakfast, as had become her habit since Amaurie refused to have breakfast in their house. Bread, milk, sometimes butter or cheese accompanied with coffee, she said very little and only complained if Amaurie asked her not to clean.

'My husband says I should do it, so I do,' was her answer to most things. She always cleaned the house thoroughly except for the cobwebs that hung in their thousands from the rafters creating one dense mass of web that filled the whole of the space in between the open rafters. These she left on purpose because spiders, like toads and lizards, keep the flies and mosquitoes down.

Carlos' wife left as she came, without a smile, in the same way she did everything, dutifully fulfilling her marital vows, looking after the children, cleaning the house, repairing clothes, gathering fruit or walking five kilometres to the ration store to get the week's rations.

The sun was already hot, well into the mid thirties, and it was only mid morning when Carlos and two of his cousins turned up with two pairs of goggles and one spear gun, between them, to go fishing.

'Catfish live on the river bed,' explained Carlos, 'to catch them you need to push them towards whoever has the spear gun, they are nearly blind so you will see them before they see you, as long as you are near to the riverbed. The best fishing is in the cave, pitch black, but as soon as you see one grab it by the tail or stick your fingers in its mouth and take it to the surface, they don't fight for long. Look,' and Carlos showed the end of his little finger was missing.

'They have little teeth but this one was a big fish, 40 lbs and a metre in length, we divided it between five families and still had a feast each!'

By now they had reached the river, which flowed in a deep valley with trees rising out on either bank, high up the side of the mountain-like slopes. Other villagers were swimming and playing by the foot of the bridge. The only girl there, she was about 13, was being teased and tormented by all the boys. Though obviously used to it she gave as good as she got and didn't hesitate to use her sharp claw-like nails; a couple of younger boys left the water with blood running down their cheeks, but they thought it was a price worth paying for having felt her breasts.

'She needs a fiancé,' said Carlos' cousin, pointing at the black haired girl with her smooth swarthy skin and delicate deep brown eyes. 'She shouldn't be fighting her own fights, it would calm the *muchachos* down too, to know that she was with someone. It isn't right.'

'You only say that because you want some, look at her, a ripe fresh mango, I bet you think of her while you are having sex with your wife.' And all the men laughed.

The fishing was fun but unsuccessful. One of Carlos' cousins narrowly missed spearing another one, who got a graze from the tip of the spear. Carlos reckoned he did it on purpose and the two men didn't speak all the way back to the village, probably disappointed by the lack of success more than anything. Carlos insisted on Amaurie eating with his family as his wife had made cheese with bamba fruit jam and galettes. They ate well in the village every night: beans, rice, vegetables; carrots, cabbage or okra, yucca or potatoes. Much better than you eat in the city which is nearly always a snack of pizza at lunchtime or a sandwich. Some of the food was provided by the government but most home produced or from the forest.

Amaurie went to bed that night, after a bout of diarrhoea, probably the well water, but he still had to drink. However he managed to fall into a deep sleep, the day had tired him out and the continuous runs were draining his energy.

His dreams were full of swamps and shooting stars when suddenly he awoke to a frightening crash. He ran out front to look and could see in the moonlight the tractor on its side, bouncing on the spot as its big rear wheel was kicking and turning against the earth, trying to get upright again. Then with a startling mechanical clunk something gave way and the great machine gave up and died. The two drivers, or rather one driver, one passenger jumped from the top side door and fled into the distance staggering and scrambling about as they fell, trying to get home. Amaurie turned round to see the damage. Three of the five posts supporting the patio were now lying in the front garden underneath the tractor, all that was left were three low stumps at ground level. The patio roof was nearly touching the ground and at one end supported only by the two remaining posts. Amaurie went back to bed.

4: WORK

By the time Amaurie got up, the tractor had been removed and about ten men from the village were standing, tools at hand, ready to repair the damage. They said nothing of the incident, no one was harmed therefore no fingers were pointed, everyone had their suspicions but kept them to themselves.

Three men began chiselling out the remains of the posts, others were repairing the thatched palm with new leaves. Some of Carlos' cousins were bringing new posts and preparing the trellis ready to put the posts back into position. By the afternoon the patio was repaired and, except for the light green leaves among the sun bleached ones of the original thatched palm, you could hardly tell the difference.

'Shame about the tractor though,' said Carlos eventually while four of the men were asleep on the patio floor worn out by the heat.

'It was our last one. Come and see.' They both climbed on the ox-drawn carriage and trundled away through the village, over the river and towards the sugar factory on the horizon. About half-way they stopped at what looked like a scrapyard but only stocked tractors and tractor parts.

'15 tractors, all Russian. We've kept them going as long as we can but we can't get the parts, it's the blockade you see, no-one will import the parts for the tractors. We need new pistons, alternators, starter motors . . . we can't repair these, you see. Look at them – 15 good machines made useless by such simple things. Now all we have left is this.' And he pointed at his strong brown biceps.

'This and our ox. That was the last tractor.' He paused to spit, but not in disgust, just to cough up some tar from the very strong cigarettes he always smoked. He looked at the anvil shaped cloud on the horizon and nodded his head towards it:

'We'd better get a move on, let's untie these oxen.'

They unhooked the cart and pushed the big beasts into the field for pasture. Slowly, reluctantly, wilfully, the animals plodded into the field chewing on the grass as they went.

'You will have to start helping us soon if you want to stay in the village.'

'Sure – what do you want me to do? I have never done much manual labour but I'm ready to learn.'

'We need everybody in the fields when we begin to collect the sugar cane. El Jefe will be coming to supervise the work and without any tractors that'll be ten times more than usual for us to do.'

'I don't have any papers. I was robbed in Havana and they took my papers,' Amaurie lied.

'That'll explain the bruising on your face when you first got here.'

'Yes,' Amaurie said, almost apologetically. He hated lying to these people but he couldn't afford to tell the truth, not that he didn't trust them, only if someone went to town and got drunk and the police overheard them, he may have difficulties.

'You can work without those for a while, if El Jefe says anything I'll say you're on holiday and helping out, let's get a move on, it's starting to rain.'

The storm lasted three days. Three days of dark cloud and continuous rain. The streets flooded then the houses flooded, a red stream of muddy water ran through his house and out into the back yard, everyone went about barefoot and carried their shoes around their necks. Most stayed indoors waiting for it to pass, patiently, expectantly, frustratedly.

In the house Amaurie placed his few possessions on the chairs, beds, shelves or the table and though he swept the water out each night, the house was flooded again the following day.

His only bag had been sitting on the corner of the bed for a few days, now empty except for a few scraps of paper. As he sat there listening to the growing storm outside, the thunder rattled the shack and the vibrations in the floor seemed to make the rocking chairs roll back and forth. He thought he saw the bag move. A rat? He cautiously opened the rucksack, machete in hand, still not sure whether he was imagining what he saw. A small, furry face stared back at him, he nearly jumped out of his skin . . . at a second glance he realised it was a small black puppy that was trembling because of the storm.

'There, there,' he said offering the dog his hand. The dog licked it and Amaurie held the little animal up against his cheek. It was a half tan and half black dog so Amaurie decided to call it Mulatto.

By the third day the storm had ended but the tension in the villagers was tangible. He could hear arguments coming from even the most distant house. Carlos had been shouting at his wife, who in turn had been shouting at the children, all through the previous night. Three days without leaving the house and Amaurie was irritable. He took it out on the pig in the back garden which he kept slapping on the bum with the flat of the machete, and wasn't content until he got a loud, high pitched squeal.

But now the sun shone again and people were going into the street to talk to each other. Mostly the conversations were about what they had been watching on TV for the last three days. Some of the youngsters were dancing, alone or in couples, not listening to the music just happy to move and communicate with their strong young bodies.

Carlos, his uncle, two cousins and a friend came to fetch Amaurie.

'Here,' said Carlos, throwing a pair of rubber boots at Amaurie's feet. This is the first human voice that had spoken to Amaurie in three days and he was glad to hear anything.

'Put these on, we have to work.'

Amaurie slipped on the boots quickly, grateful for something to do, grabbed his machete and followed the men onto the back of the ox-drawn cart where five other men were already sitting. After an hour or so of slow travelling along the steaming dirt track, and lots of chatter, mainly about the 13-year-old Lolita that most of the men were fantasising about, they reached the edge of the huge sugarcane fields that stood tall, above the height of a man. The light green fields stretched on towards the horizon and beyond. Some paths had already been cut through the dense green cane and horses and donkeys stood with bundles of cane strapped to their backs. There could have been as many as a hundred men working in the fields; none could be seen but everywhere for about half a mile the ends of the cane branches trembled and flickered and the rhythmical sound of machetes, hacking at the thick base of the plants, could be heard. As the sun went down most men were exhausted yet connected with the day's work. They felt a certain contentedness at achieving a man's work. They had done the work of five tractors and in less time than was expected. They had achieved this through solidarity and a single sense of purpose. And though later, round a bottle of rum, they would complain that all this work for 20 Cuban *pesos* a day is akin to slavery, they felt like men that day, Cuban men, patriots who once again had fought for the revolution, and though the war against imperialism will one day come to an end, they felt they had won this battle. They had beaten the blockade by sheer strength of will. As have the Cuban people ever since the Revolution.

When he got back to the village 'Lolita' (that was the nickname

Amaurie gave the young girl of the village) was standing behind a tree near his house.

'*Hola que tal?*'

'*Bien chica, y tu* . . . Why are you standing alone out here?'

'Oh, I'm avoiding the boys in the village. I need some peace.'

'What about me?'

'Oh, you're a man. I don't mind men,' she said coquettishly.

They spent the hour flirting with each other. Lolita was interested to know about Havana and the big city she'd seen on TV. He told her all about the salsa clubs, Malecon, the mojito bars, the big hotels and, of course, the American cars.

'How old do girls start having sex?' she asked with counterfeited naivety.

'When they're ready,' he answered honestly.

'I was eleven,' she confessed flirtatiously, slowly closing and opening her eyes like a drowsy cat.

He knew what she wanted and surprised himself by walking her home. Most of the way to her shack she spoke of marriage and living in the big city, she didn't want to start having children when she was 15, like her sister, she wanted to live a bit more. Like all teenage girls she wanted a knight in shining armour to come along and take her away to some golden palace where all is peaceful and fun.

Amaurie needed to get away. He had to change his money and see if he could get a boat to America. He'd probably get enough to pay for the trip to Miami, but he didn't have any contacts there. He'd have to go back to Havana and see who he could meet to help him find a boat, someone he could trust. He knew what the people are like in Havana and even a friend of a friend will make false promises for $500. His best friend was dead and his regular girlfriend was probably not going to be happy to see him after all this time. He needed money to get to Havana and would have to change some of his foreign currency. Without his ID card he couldn't do this. The only person he trusted was El Viejo. He'd have to tell more lies and deceive this kind old man, but he didn't have any choice. He decided to talk to the village elder tomorrow and ask him for help.

As he walked Lolita home to the other side of the village she held his hand tightly. Nobody could see them in the dark so this little indiscretion would not lead to any trouble. Amaurie enjoyed the small hand of this young woman, small strong and yet soft and malleable in his own, a hand that had done few of the womanly chores she would be expected to do when she married.

They walked past El Zonzon's house and he was snoring away in front of the TV that was blaring out more anti-American propaganda. In the house next to Lolita's the whole family sat watching a noisy American action movie, the only entertainment in the village and the talking point for the next few days.

He kissed Lolita, or rather she kissed him, good night and strolled back to his shack, hands in pockets, pondering his next move and searching the sky for shooting stars.

5: THE FIGHT

'OK, the day after tomorrow we'll get the *guagagitta* and go into town. I'll change the money for you my friend.'

Amaurie was surprised to hear of a bus – this was the first time anyone in the village had mentioned it and he had never seen a bus come through that way.

Anyway he was grateful for the old man's kindness and said that he had told a lie about his ailing mother, whom he could never see because she was probably being observed by the police right now and maybe forever or until he could get news to her from America.

When he left the old man's house he noticed El Zonzon standing on the other side of the street staring at the same front door Amaurie had just closed behind himself.

'It's a shame when friends don't speak,' began El Zonzon, surprisingly sober for once. 'We fell out nearly 30 years ago now. When he went with the faithful to the Bay of Pigs, and I stayed behind.'

'Well one day you will speak again,' Amaurie said optimistically.

'Hmmm, well are you coming to the forest?' As he couldn't think of anything else to do he followed El Zonzon slowly along the dirt track and over the river.

There were many *muchachos* in the forest and they were all excited, milling around, pushing and shoving each other in an agitation that was unusual for these youths who usually spent their time fishing or watching TV.

A few hundred yards away a wild groaning could be heard and the bushes and trees shook and trembled in a particular patch of the dense undergrowth. It couldn't be a bear, surely not a crocodile, whatever it was it wasn't human and it was half wild, perhaps a bull, Amaurie thought to himself. The men moved on into a clearing where a few logs had been felled to make seats. Here, some of the older men from the village sat chatting, sharing a bottle of rum talking quickly with eager short phrases, almost running out of breathe as they gabbled. They too were as excited as the younger men. All was a tense sense of apprehension. Something was about to happen.

Then, from the other side of the thick woodland to where the animal noise was coming from, a crowd of about ten or fifteen boys came running, aged between twelve and eighteen, in the middle of the gang and dragging along the eldest boy on the end of a lead was a large well-set pit bull. From the scars on the dog's face and its torn ears this wasn't its first fight.

The other dog, for such it was, now became more agitated, jumping in the air and being pulled short by the rope that tied it to a tree. The older men started placing bets on the dogs while the boys began clearing the pit and scoring the line.

'50 *pesos* on the ginger dog,' one of them cried out.

'I'll match that for Jolie, he's won every fight he's had, never seen a dog like it, even killed two other dogs.'

'Ah, but he's past it, look how much bigger Ginger is, I saw him kill a mongrel yesterday just by standing on it, that's a big dog!'

By now the men were getting more excited. The two dogs had seen each other and were pulling and yapping and growling so hard it took three boys to hold each dog, otherwise the fight would have started too soon. The dogs snarled and bounced, jumping at each other before being tugged back to the ground, the physical strength and eagerness to fight was astounding. The bets had been placed and the dogs were brought into the ring. No-one stood in between them. The first bite went deep into Jolie's collar and blood started oozing down his neck onto his chest. The ginger dog fought hard.

Amaurie saw the silver flash of a switch blade and the blood poured from his friend's throat like wine from a spilt chalice. There was nothing he could do but throw his own knife in the face of the gang leader from Habana Vieja and run. His last view of Miguel had been his body lying there in a pool of blood. The other gang members were after Amaurie now.

The vision of his dying friend and so much blood made him want to cry. At that moment just as Ginger had Jolie by the throat, the clouds opened with one of the frequent storms. Amaurie used this as an excuse to go; he already had a cold and didn't want it to get worse. The other men didn't take much notice they were shouting and jeering like demented football fans who have forgotten even why they are shouting in the first place.

The road home was peaceful and Amaurie was grateful for the rain as it concealed his tears.

6: LA GAUGAGITTA

As the sun came up over the misty sugarcane fields people started to walk to the centre of the village, slowly and mysteriously as though going to some sort of cult worship, almost somnambulant. Some children were playing in the broken down wreck of the bus. El Viejo had been waiting patiently outside Amaurie's house, who offered coffee.

'He's late,' complained the old man, 'another half an hour and I will go and get him, lazy drunk, this bus should have left three days ago.'

Amaurie still didn't understand; where was the bus? Where was the driver? When did the bus come through the village? El Viejo began to loose patience and walked into the village huffing and moaning about the bus driver. Then he just stood there and shouted:

'Are you going to get up, you lazy drunk, or do I have to come in and fetch you?'

By the time El Viejo returned to join Amaurie the door opened in a nearby house and a middle-aged man, with a large belly and a hangover, wearing no top, staggered out. He walked as far as the gate, stooped down, rubbed his hands in morning dew then rinsed his face, brushed back his hair and with a grizzly voice said:

'*Buena dia*,' to the expecting crowd, now about nine or ten of them. He then clambered on board the old wreck of the bus.

There were few windows left on the small, twenty-seater bus. The windscreen was cracked and most of the seats were broken or missing. Everyone watched expectantly as the driver lifted off the cover of the engine, turned some nuts with a spanner, took off the air filter and blew into it. Then he siphoned some diesel into the fuel pump, switched a switch, pulled a lever and turned the key. Nothing. He went through the process again, this time with the help of one of the tractor mechanics, who had heard all the fuss and decided to come and help. Still nothing. The *muchachos* on the bus were finding it amusing to pull the wings off flying insects and throw the wriggling bodies down Lolita's cleavage, which in turn made her wriggle and scream a lot.

Suddenly a cloud of exhaust fumes billowed out of the engine as it made a loud bang. The mechanic kept twisting and pulling bolts and levers and the engine kept running to the sound of a loud chug, chug. Very shortly the whole bus was filled with exhaust fumes. The passengers choked and smiled as the bus slowly backed out of the gully. Then everything came to a standstill.

'You'll have to get off and push,' said the driver uninterestedly. He would rather the bus didn't work, then he could stay at home.

Everyone got off, waited for the engine to start again, listened for the crunching sound of the reverse gear, and then they pushed. The whole rescue attempt was unorganised; someone was even pushing from behind until he realised that the bus was going backwards. With one mighty shove and a jolt the bus heaved its way out of the ditch and reversed up onto the dusty, red dirt track. It changed gear and pulled off while people were still clambering aboard. Fortunately El Viejo had had the good sense to remain on *la guaga*.

The bus carried on for another half kilometre on the same track, then suddenly turned and crashed straight into the jungle. Evidently this was the path it usually took because they didn't hit a tree once. But for many kilometres branches and huge banana or palm leaves smacked against the side of the bus, sometimes reaching in and slapping an unexpecting passenger on the face. Every few kilometres the bus broke free from the forest, jumped out and bounced over a track that ran through a sugarcane field.

The noise inside and out was too loud to allow any form of conversation. The bus driver and mechanic communicated with hand signals and everyone else just shouted without being heard. El Viejo sat patiently on one of the few unbroken seats, and two hours later *la guaga* pulled into the rundown town built up around the sugar factory.

It was already 11 am and Amaurie had to get to the bank by 4 pm. This meant he had to find a lift quickly. After half an hour of waiting in the blazing sunlight a lorry pulled up and some young men who'd been standing around jumped in the back. El Viejo started to make for the ladder welded to the back of the lorry, but Amaurie pulled him back, he was too old to travel 150 miles in the back of an open top lorry in this heat. El Viejo didn't put up much resistance. Anyway now most of the hitchers had gone they were the first in the queue. Another 45 minutes standing in the heat of the sun, El Viejo was sitting in an open doorway a few metres further on, trying to stay in the shade, it must have been well into the top thirties even where he sat. Amaurie was giving up hope.

Slowly over the dusty track where vision was impaired by the heat rising and transforming the world into a gaseous substance, something started to materialise. It sounded like a tractor, with a radio blaring out country and western. The sunlight almost dazzled Amaurie as it shone off the huge chrome front guard and bumper of the sky blue Cadillac as it pulled up in front of him. El Viejo stood up, walked to the car and ran his fingers along the shiny wings, up the silver edged window screen, over the roof and down the back of the car. Amaurie was discussing with the driver if they were going anywhere near the nearest bank. As he was talking the old man climbed into the back of the car and sat down with a huge grin. He didn't mind where the car was going.

The driver, with his family, wife, three kids, father and uncle, drove fifty kilometres out of his way to take Amaurie to the bank on time. As the shiny metallic monster grumbled and trundled off into the shimmering distance, Amaurie turned to the old man and gave him forty dollars. A few minutes later they were back on the road again, trying to hitch a lift back to the *guagagitta* that usually left around 8 pm, depending on how drunk the driver and the mechanic were. Most bars refused to serve them but sometimes they remembered to take a bottle of El Zonzon's home-made rum with them.

The two very weary travellers missed the bus.

At around midnight, El Viejo asleep in the back of the cart, and Amaurie clinging onto two huge plastic milk urns, the two friends finally made it home.

7: THE MOVE

Mulato had crapped in the kitchen, by the door. Amaurie had completely forgotten about the dog when he left the house in the morning. The animal was getting quite big now and would make a formidable guard dog, once fully grown, if there was anything to guard against.

His stomach was burning as usual as he woke up the following day. He should have bought some bottled water when he was in town, but he must save his money. Amaurie didn't know when he'd be paid for work again. It was getting vital that he travelled up to Havana to find out about a boat. He didn't care where he got the crossing to, maybe Jamaica and then America, but he couldn't live in Cuba forever, waiting to be arrested every time he set foot out of the village.

El Viejo was becoming a good friend and they would sit and chat, or rather Amaurie would listen while El Viejo spoke about his 90 years (and sometimes more!) in the village. Amaurie didn't want to speak much about himself. He didn't want to lie anymore.

'I went to Playa Giron to meet Fidel, hundreds of us did. Not many got that far. By the time I got there Fidel was on his way to Havana and Ché had already taken Santiago. Four years I spent in the anti-Imperialistic forces, mainly trying to stop wealthy Cubans fleeing to America once their property had been seized. The Gringos we let go. Four years then I came back here to work the sugar plantation. Just like the others. Still got no school, no doctor, no transport, even the tractors have packed up now. I'd like to say it is the blockade but now, after all these years, I think we've simply been forgotten. A little village, with a few inhabitants, who in the world cares about us. We've been making our own tools and fending for ourselves for years. None of these big American skyscrapers or doctors with computers here. Most of us have only ever seen a computer on TV, I still don't know what they do, don't suppose I ever will. Do you?'

'No,' lied Amaurie, who couldn't be bothered to explain. Somewhere inside he felt it was time for change so he changed the subject.

'When is Carlos' cousin moving to Havana?'

'Day after next. You'll get a lift to Havana then. Now make me a coffee on that old paraffin stove Josè's wife gave you.'

The day went on and most of the talk was about the village. Another family leaving the village. Another empty house. Soon be no children left. He'll have to pick up the lorry, maybe travel into town the night before.

By 11 pm on the day of the move Carlos' cousin turned up with the lorry. Although he'd officially booked the hire of the lorry months ago *El Jefe* of the renting of transport service in town needed the lorry to deliver a car the following day. Carlos' cousin wasn't allowed the use of the lorry so he borrowed it anyway. He had to get to Havana and back by the following day without being stopped by the police because he didn't have the written permission to use the lorry and he couldn't afford a bribe.

Straight away the big man, built like an ox, began to sling his belongings into the back of the lorry while his wife and some of the villagers stood and watched. Amaurie wanted to help but he'd eaten too much and his diarrhoea was so bad that every time he lifted something he felt it seeping out. Not only that but the initial strain of lifting a table and cupboard brought on a fever that made his legs weak. All he could manage were a couple of light bags with clothes in them; all the clothes the family owned.

By 3 am the lorry was clunking along the dirt track on its way to Havana 233 kilometres away. The family of Carlos' cousin, Carlos, the wife, her mother and three kids sat in the front of the lorry. The four other passengers stood among the badly stacked furniture in the back, taking it in turns to hold the mirror so as to avoid seven years without sex that a broken mirror would have cursed them with.

The men in the back, including Amaurie, smoked and chatted. It was a warm night and fortunately it didn't rain. They also took it in turns sitting on the little floor space there was. Amaurie wished he hadn't eaten today every time the lorry hit a pot-hole and jolted, about every five minutes, he thought he was going to mess himself.

As they rolled down the back streets of Havana they could already feel the heat of the sun, everyone on the look out for police check points in case they had to do a u-turn and find another way into Havana. The flat was on the outskirts of Havana and had cost 18,000 Cuban *pesos*. Nobody asked where the money came from and nobody cared.

As they began to unload Amaurie made his excuses and found a convenient bush in the park behind which he could relieve himself.

Then he headed off towards Buena Vista and Habana Vieja. The roads were dusty and a low level smog of diesel and nut oil fumes hung around the feet of pedestrians. At every traffic light queues of people waited for a lift into town: school children, office workers, shop assistants, community workers all waited hopefully in the morning sun that was already too hot for most people, who sat in the shade. Some of the women were fanning themselves with lace fans that looked as though they'd been hand made in Spain. The girls stood there well dressed and smiling hopefully at every Chevrolet, Dodge, Buick or Lada that rolled past. Most of the cars stopped to ask where the prospective passengers might be going and some of the hitchers got in.

Amaurie had almost forgotten what the pace was like in the big city and his awareness of everything seemed to be made even more acute by his sickness. Or perhaps, during most of his adult life in Havana, he'd been drunk or had a hangover. He couldn't remember getting up this early before, though he'd often been going home at this time.

Home, he'd have to avoid his home. The police may still be on the look out for him and they would definitely be observing his mother's house. He'd like to get a message to her though and he had to get in touch with his girlfriend's uncle. The first thing he needed was some medicine though.

He went to the polyclinic that sold drugs to tourists, that way he could buy some pain killers and something to stop the diarrhoea, even though he knew the best thing was not to eat.

By the time he'd got the medicine and arranged to meet Maria's uncle it was already getting dark. At 10 pm Maria would be going to Malecon. He wanted to see her even if it was just to say goodbye, and he knew how unhappy she'd be when her uncle told her he'd been to Havana, if they didn't see each other.

Los muchachos were driving slowly along, elbows on windowless doors, ragaton blasting from speakers, whistling, hooting or shouting at the pretty *muchachas* who lined the promontory. The sea was breaking on the rocks behind the wall and, as the wind picked up, a cool wisp of fine sea spray could be felt on the back of his neck as he walked along. A group of girls sat huddled on the wall, waiting eagerly for something to happen, namely they were waiting for boys to sing to them or take them along the street dancing. Maria was sitting there cheerful but evidently half-bored, half-expecting someone. Amaurie had to get her away from the other girls, he had to get her attention. He stood nearby waiting for the other girls to be distracted when, to his surprise, she jumped off the wall and walked away determinedly. He followed her closely and as she stopped to cross the road he pulled at her T-shirt sleeve. She turned in a start and then giggled, expecting someone else, she didn't recognise him straight away but then when a car light lit up his eyes she realised who it was.

'*Hola*,' he said.

'I didn't recognise you, you've lost weight, you look like an old man, where have you been?'

They got a taxi to a bar the other side of town in a tourist street of Havana Vieja where it was unlikely anyone would recognise him. He could afford mojitos and Maria enjoyed them too. She told him all that had happened. She'd been kept in for questioning for seven hours after the fight. Only Miguel was dead and everyone went to the funeral. The police were everywhere, she'd finished college now and was waiting for a work placement and ... '*y amigo-mio*,' she said and softly and deliberately placed her hand on the table, palm down. The sparkle of a diamond, so fine almost like dust, glistened on the silver ring. Amaurie was a little taken back, and felt it out of place and too hypocritical to say

104

congratulations. She could have been his if he'd tried a little harder and kept out of trouble. Deep inside he felt happy for her. She was already twenty-two and he knew she felt almost past the sell by date.

They went back to Malecon and had sex for one last time. The sexual energy still remained between them but the friendship was dying out. He wished he could take her dancing but he still had one thing to do before the meeting with her uncle. He didn't tell Maria about the meeting or the boat. He just said he'd be going back to the village.

He caught a cocotaxi to the cemetery and paid a dollar, anything more was a rip off and the driver seemed to agree and sped off quite happily. The cemetery was locked but Amaurie had broken in there on numerous occasions. As he walked past the white marble angels and ornamental tombs the reality of Miguel's death brought tears to his eyes. He finally found the small grey stone monument, exactly where Maria had described it to be, he knelt down and for the first time in his life he said a prayer. He prayed for Miguel's soul, that it may rest in peace, and he prayed for his own soul that it may one day learn to fly.

The meeting with Maria's uncle, a lawyer by profession, didn't take long. They met by a sandwich bar near the Ministry of Communication.

'Here's the deal,' explained the lawyer. 'You pay 400 dollars now and 400 dollars once you're on the boat. Go to Cien Fuegos and wait by the beach two kilometres to the west. You may have to wait three or four days. You'll know the boat by its red light at the top of the mast, no other colour. Once the light turns white and heads for shore get yourself to the beach as quick as possible, you'll have to swim out to the boat and there will be other people there. But only those with names on the list will be allowed on board. Don't tell anyone your real name until you get on the boat, and keep away from the police.'

'I will, don't you worry,' said Amaurie, handing over the paper folder with the money.

'Y suerte,' said the older man squeezing him firmly by the hand. 'May God protect you.'

Amaurie turned his back on Havana with relief. This old capital city, a city like Paris, Madrid, London, New York, Rome, Barcelona, any major capital city where cars rush by and people hardly have the time of day. The only thing that talks in Havana and everybody talks about is money. If you're not negotiating you're not talking. Unless you are talking love, that is, but even then you have to be able to take a *chica* out and pay for her to go dancing.

It was with relief that Amaurie jumped off the same dusty old cart onto the same dusty old track in the same dusty old village that he had found nearly six months previously. He took some more painkillers and went to bed. Nobody seemed to notice him come in but the shutters of his elderly neighbour's shack were soon pushed open like a kindly eye waking up to see a friend return.

8: HOME IS WHERE THE HEART IS

The fever lasted three days and three nights and that in spite of the painkillers and the anti-diarrhoea treatment. The time spent in Havana had been exhausting. Although the journey back had been a lot less strenuous, Amaurie knew where he was going this time, it had still been long and tiring in the heat.

El Viejo had been bringing him tea three times a day, though he hardly noticed because of his hallucinogenic state. At one point he'd got up to talk to a large purple iguana that was standing on the porch asking directions to the nearest banana plantation. The iguana was bigger than a cat and as big as most dogs. Sweat poured into his eyes as he watched the reptile wander off on its way. Carlos' wife had changed his sheets for him when they were soaked with sweat. He only just managed to muster up enough energy to get to the latrine to avoid messing his bed. When the sickness came over him too all he did was lie by the hole in the ground, waiting to be sick. His body flushed cold and hot every ten minutes. Occasionally he just drifted in and out of his conscious state, neither sleeping nor awake.

When he finally came around to normality he could hear the sound of a child or a cat slowly being tortured. He knew what was happening, someone nearby was slaughtering a goat. The animal screamed as its two hind legs were tied to separate branches and its throat was slit. Slowly, as it bled to death the goat quietened and settled. It was quickly gutted and skinned and put into the pot before the flies could get to it.

'It's for a wake,' El Viejo said mournfully.

At first Amaurie didn't understand and thought that these strange country people were having a wake for the very animal they had just killed.

'El Zonzon died the day before yesterday. At least we think it was then, nobody had seen him for five days,' explained El Viejo.

'Three days ago someone heard him shouting blue murder, but put it down to him being drunk again. It must have been his liver. Eventually someone asked me to go and look, I found him stretched out on the floor his arms straight above his head. Rigor mortis had already set in. We had to break his arms to get him on the stretcher and onto the cart to take him to the cemetery. Tonight we will have a wake in his place, then we will decide what to do with his things. His rum still will be hotly disputed for. Do you want to come?'

In spite of the pain of digesting food Amaurie ate some of the Fruta Bomba marmalade and bread that Carlos' wife had put out for him. He went into the backyard where the chickens were running about and clucking merrily, heated some water from the well and washed all over. The fresh water did him good.

The wake went well. The people managed to finish off Zonzon's last few bottles of rum and Amaurie felt a lot better after half a bottle. He even found the energy to dance with Lolita, who was over the moon, because most of the men in the village didn't dance very well.

The goat meat was good, though he knew he was going to regret eating it, so too was the chicken, the rice and the beans, the yucca and everything else that the villagers brought for the feast. He was half starved through not eating for so many days and diarrhoea and dysentery had left him empty.

El Viejo gave a speech about what a good man El Zonzon had been while his wife was around and how he regretted the action he took that broke their friendship. They hadn't spoken a word for nearly thirty years now. He recalled how before becoming a drunk El Zonzon was a hard worker in the plantations, he was always ready to help those less fortunate than himself and was an honest and sincere man.

The moon was up in the sky now and nightjars and parrots squawked in the crepuscular forest. The huge leaves of the banana trees fanned backward and forwards in the warm evening breeze. Amaurie smiled to himself, in spite of the pain in his stomach. He felt at home. In Zonzon's house men were still arguing about who got possession of, and how to use, the still. The still had been made using copper imported by the Russians in the times when they still had new tractors.

It was a fifteen-kilometre walk to the cemetery. The women and children went by trailer cart while most of the men walked. There was lots of laughing and joking about El Zonzon, about his drunkenness and the scrapes he'd managed to get into. Few remembered what he was like thirty years ago before the rum got the better of him.

Amaurie was a little surprised that the drunkard was given a Catholic burial, a very elaborate ceremony with full communion for many of the villagers.

El Zonzon buried, and their souls replenished, the group of people then turned and walked the fifteen kilometres back to the village in the burning sun. It was about 37° in the shade and the heat rose from the path and swallowed the women and children as they rode off into the distance.

The villagers seemed at peace with themselves now the mourning was over, it left a sense of shared community. Another one had moved on and another will be born in his place was the attitude, that is how it was and that is how it will be. They couldn't see any radical change on its way nor had they ever noticed any. Life goes on and necessity gives them the means to keep going. Amaurie wanted to do something for El Zonzon and decided to pay for his headstone. The stone cutter had just finished the work on the small tablet of marble: Jésus Ferdinand Rodriguez 1917–2007. The young man was surprised to see the drunkard's real name and sat down to contemplate it. How much he must have seen during his 90 years on earth. What changes, people coming, people going, what suffering he must have felt to drive him to thirty years of alcohol abuse. His only companion during his lonely existence was a bottle of rum. Yet still he remained part of the village, considered a drunken fool by most, and used as an example to frighten children, even though he was accepted as part of the village and everyone turned out to pay their respects.

'Who would come to my funeral?' Amaurie asked himself.

'How surprised they would be to see my real name on a headstone. As long as I live this lie I can't really fit in anywhere. Maybe it will be different in America.'

9: THE ARREST

He was almost relieved by the dull, rhythmical thud, thud, thud, pause thud, thud, thud, on the door. By now he was completely off food. Six months of nearly constant diarrhoea had taken its toll. He had the energy to move around the house and make an infusion but anything more than that left him exhausted. Most of the day he lay in bed or sat in the rocking chair on the porch watching the world slowly go by. The pain in his stomach was sometimes crippling and he wasn't surprised that he had an ulcer, his stomach lining was badly torn and he'd been shitting blood for a week.

The police let themselves in and helped him out of bed. The handcuffs seemed to weigh like an anvil around his wrists as they lead him to the van further along the red dirt track. The villagers lined the road to watch him go, this was a sight few of them had ever seen before, two police cars, ten policemen and an armoured van, even in the town there was never so much police presence.

The tribunal was quick to pass judgement, the trial had already been discussed in full and held in his absence. The sentence was limited because of lack of evidence. The knife had never been found and the one in Amaurie's possession didn't match the forensic records. He was sentenced to five years imprisonment for possession of a dangerous weapon in a public place. By now Amaurie was beyond caring. He didn't think he was going to live much longer and didn't much feel like living. At least he got to see his mother sooner than he thought and she visited him once a month in prison.

After a few weeks on a drip in the prison hospital he started to get his energy back. He soon learnt to keep his head down and out of trouble. It was especially important not to be noticed by the guards, they reacted quickly and brutally to anything they considered abnormal, they were always ready to remind the inmates who was boss.

One of his cell mates had been given eight years for manslaughter after defending himself from a drunken stepfather. He was on an education programme for young, short term inmates and was training to be a lawyer. The other cell mate had been given twenty years for repeatedly robbing tourists.

Once he'd got his strength back and got into the routine of prison life he signed up to learn organic farming. He thought this would be useful once he returned to the village.

Twice a week he was let out of prison to tend the organic allotment nearby. He was still having trouble digesting food and found it ironic that most of the food he was producing would only irritate his damaged stomach. Still it got him out and it was with a deep sigh he breathed in the fresh air of the free world.

Once every few months El Viejo would come to visit. God knows how the old man would travel the two-hundred-kilometre round trip, and only through the will of God (according to El Viejo) did he make it each time. But Amaurie was grateful for these visits and the news of the village was mostly petty gossip but it kept him entertained and gave him something to look forward to. Still no spares for the tractors, everybody was ploughing the fields by ox and horse. The schoolteacher had run off with the doctor and both had been posted elsewhere. Now there was no-one to teach the children and no-one to cure them. Mulato was now bigger than any of the fighting dogs and just as impressive. Carlos' wife had run off with Carlos' cousin then after a big fight she returned. But otherwise things were the same.

'People come and people go but the village remains the same,' said the wise old man.

Amaurie was grateful for this news from home, the little incidents that he could relate to with his heart stood in contrast with the cold and inhuman surroundings of the prison.

Then the visits stopped. Amaurie asked his mother to go to the village to find out why the old man hadn't been to see him for 18 months. He tried phoning the sugar factory to see if he could get any news. It would take his mother months to find the time to get there and she didn't want to travel alone.

By the time he was released he had received his diploma in organic farming. He had also become quite good in a fight. A couple of scars on his forearm showed where he'd had to defend himself, mainly from the guards. His hands were now strong from all the manual work he'd been doing. He was given a lift to Havana, his last official residence, but didn't hang around for long.

10: EL HABANERO

The cart trundled away along the dark ochre track that ran along the edge of the forest. He looked up and down the road, the only road in and out of the village. The sun was setting and women were rinsing the beans or preparing the meat in front of the houses, getting ready for the meal. A few houses away a new shack had sprung up, with a corrugated tin roof and a modern external light. Under the light Lolita stood, babe in arms and a toddler by her side, still with the same vacant expectant look she had on her face as when he had last seen her.

A big black and tan dog sat on the porch in front of the door and growled as Amaurie approached. The middle aged man, now slightly greying, sat in the rocking chair and stretched out his hand:

'*Venga para aqui Mulato,*' he ordered in a gentle voice.

The strong dog slowly stood, its tail between its legs, and walked towards the man. The dog's ears had been torn and its left eye had almost scarred closed. The dog was happy to see the man. He gently licked Amaurie's hand as though licking an old wound that had healed over a long time ago but its memory brought back pain. Amaurie patted its strong square head deliberately each time a little harder than before until the tail went from a nervous uncertain twitch to a full and jovial wag as the whole of the back end of the dog moved from side to side.

In the back yard a toad croaked and this made Amaurie laugh. He stood up to look at the overgrown garden at his neighbour's house, but the wooden shutters were closed tightly and no light shone beyond them.

As he slowly pushed open the door to the house the hinges creaked and groaned. Bright, white, light filtered in rays through the dust particles that span constantly around the room. He battered the dust from his bed and lay down. The large black dog kept guard at the foot of the bed.

A cock crowed before daylight then another an hour later. Amaurie lay there listening to the sounds of the country. The coo of a wild dove echoed through the trees accompanied by the high pitched squawk of a parrot, other birds whistled in harmony and the melodious polyphonies were only broken by the squeal of a piglet and the sound of passing horses.

Once he'd washed himself using the bucket in the garden, he got dressed and walked barefoot through the village. The warm damp soil stuck to the bottom of his feet, he stooped to pick up a handful and squeezed it knowingly between his fingers. The soil broke and fell in red clumps to the ground. He smiled. The village was waking up. Nobody took any notice of him as he walked by, more at home with each step he took. Nothing had changed. Some of the men nodded to him with a quick '*Hola*' as they trotted off to work with hoe slung over their shoulders. It was as though he had never been away. The morning breeze rustled the large leaves of the banana trees as he reached the plantation, flashing their yellow crop temptingly. He turned on the spot and lightly, almost skipping, strolled back through the village.

Carlos' wife brought him a glass of coffee and as he sat there watching the rising sun he had a vision. A tall dark megalith cast a shadow down the slope over the small garden, blocking the sun. Amaurie looked up and smiled.

'I can't see you but you can see me.' The voice of the vision spoke with a voice older than the world.

Amaurie jumped up, outstretched his hand and went over to the old man. It wasn't until El Viejo missed the handshake, waving his own arm aimlessly in the direction of Amaurie, that Amaurie realised he was blind.

'Here let me help you.' The younger man said leading El Viejo to the rocking chair and sitting him down.

The two friends sat talking for most of the day, each taking it in turns to pause and listen, only stopping to walk back to the banana plantation. The walk did El Viejo good.

Amaurie told the old man all about his plans to develop an organoponica in the village and organise transport and delivery of food to the nearby town.

'We'll have to find you a woman now you're back,' said the old man, very matter of fact. 'You can't have a house without a woman.'

But that was another story.

The *guagagitta* wobbled past, now bright pink with shiny silver trimming though still coughing out clouds of smoke. A group of schoolchildren scrambled off the bus in smart uniform of red shorts and red neckties. As they scuffled by all snotty with grazed knees one of the older boys called out

'*Mira, es El Habanero!*'

Amaurie knew he could stop lying now.

THE END

MY LAST FEW DAYS

After travelling 200 kilometres in the back of a lorry with sickness and diarrhoea, clenching my buttocks every time we hit a bump, trying to sleep a feverous sleep and being shaken around in the lorry, I made it to the town I was to meet Dave. All I wanted was to go to bed. Hungry but fearing to eat, I staggered into *La Casa Particular* to be told that Dave had left an urgent message.

When I got through to him he told me he'd just arrived from Mayfair but his American credit cards didn't work in Cuba so he had no money. Hence he'd checked into a top hotel in Havana and wondered if I could travel the 800 kilometres round trip to come and bail him out.

Fucking Londoners!

The next conversation: after I'd spent the whole day on the toilet making the most disgusting smells imaginable, Dave is sitting in his hotel room drinking Pimms and reading porn magazines (which are illegal in Cuba), so he was OK.

The diarrhoea continued and I was glad Dave was stuck in Havana for three days, sorting out his finances. The people in the CP told me that I didn't have the symptoms of food poisoning but I'd probably picked up a parasite from drinking the well water in the country.

I decided to try and kill the parasite. Firstly I'd starve it out then I'd knock it out. When Dave finally turned up we sat down with two bottles of rum and I began my vicious attack on the resilient creature living in my stomach.

We had a funny encounter with the local homosexual community; it turns out that there are lots of gay men in Cuba. Homosexuality is readily accepted by the state and most of the population. I even saw straight men dancing with gay men when there were no women around to dance the ladies' steps. Gays in Cuba are very gay and talk mainly about handbags. After our first night out, by the time we'd left the third nightclub Dave was a little worse for wear. Jet lag and rum had got the most of him and like a true Brit he passed out on the pavement in front of the nightclub. I tried to pick him up but he's a heavy sod when blind drunk, so I sat by him talking to a cute Irish girl we'd met earlier on the beach. As we were so engrossed in conversation I didn't notice the five gay men who had surrounded Dave and were trying to help sober him up. They were being very maternal and obviously felt sorry for him. When eventually they all managed to lift him completely off the floor and started wandering off with him I came running over shouting in Spanish:

'Leave him alone he's with me!'

They dropped him where he was and finally, with the Irish girl's help, I managed to get him to bed.

The following day every gay man in Trinidad, who had completely ignored me up until now, came up to us to say '*hola*' and shook our hands. So much for the reputation with the women.

We tried to go deep sea fishing but this was $300 a day and we decided we had better things to spend our money on. Everyday we went to the beach and it became a joke to me and Dave as we'd get up in the morning, look at each other and say, '*Vamos a la playa!*' This was the theme tune to the Cuban trip. That's really all there is to do: go to the beach. Who cares about anything else.

The rest of my stay was rum, dancing and fucking (yes I met a beautiful mulata who didn't want my money, just sex). I discovered a great drink called Un Colonial. Nobody in Havana had heard of it. I think it can only be found in Trinidad and I recommend that you go there to try it.

The following day someone turned up with a huge fish and told me it was for my leaving celebration. I stood there holding it for a few minutes, discussing with Dave what to do with it. A knock at the door and another friend turned up to tell me his cousin was a chef and that he'd sort it out. In the evening Dave and I paid for four cabs to take all my friends to the beach. It was empty and we had a great party, swimming in the sea with Dave and ten Cuban friends, floating there watching the flying fish jump in the moonlight. I said to him:

'I was born to live in the Caribbean.'

'Everyone was born to live in the Caribbean,' he replied.

FINALLY

Six weeks later I still have an upset stomach. Though I've stopped drinking rum. The rum certainly seemed to do something, I think it sedated the parasite rather than killed it. If I'm careful with what I eat (mainly rice and carrots) I'm OK. For the first few days in England I seemed OK, until I had a Full English (veggie of course) and then the diarrhoea started again. A thinks it may be a parasite called *giardia*. I'm going to see my Mum's GP in France next week because I have no confidence in the British NHS and if I'm going to be ill I may as well be ill at home.

I'm still in touch with Cuba and will be for a while. It will be interesting to see how the country changes over the next few years. Will Castro resign after the 50th anniversary of the revolution? After all he's been head of state almost as long as the Queen, and he chose to be so! The people of Cuba are ready for change too, though they don't want the guns, drugs, prostitution and exploitation that capitalism has brought to most of Latin America and the Caribbean.

I'm still planning to sail out there one day. First I'll have a go at going round Britain to practise my navigation and sailing skills, then I need to raise the funds. I know someone who pays people to sail back from Brazil with organic cocoa beans, to avoid pollution. This seems like a way forward to me, there is plenty to look forward to anyway, and life is beautiful. I'm glad I went to Cuba when I was thirty-seven!

I still haven't heard from Christina and I doubt I'll ever see her again.